CUI Reference Guide

I0095368

Select Laws, Regulations, and Government-Wide Policies Related to the United States Government's CUI Program

CUI Reference Guide: Select Laws, Regulations, and Government-Wide Policies Related to the United States Government's CUI Program

Compilation Copyright 2023 James Goepel, All Rights Reserved

1st Edition

Although the author has made every effort to ensure that the information in this book was correct at press time, the author does not assume and hereby disclaims any liability to any party for any loss, damage, or disruption caused by any errors or omissions, whether such errors or omissions result from negligence, accident, or any other cause.

To preserve the formatting and legibility of DoDI 5200.48, the headers and footers of the CUI Reference Guide have been omitted from the corresponding pages.

Contents

Executive Order 13556 -- Controlled Unclassified Information

The White House
Office of the Press Secretary
For Immediate Release

November 04, 2010

By the authority vested in me as President by the Constitution and the laws of the United States of America, it is hereby ordered as follows:

Section 1. Purpose. This order establishes an open and uniform program for managing information that requires safeguarding or dissemination controls pursuant to and consistent with law, regulations, and Government-wide policies, excluding information that is classified under Executive Order 13526 of December 29, 2009, or the Atomic Energy Act, as amended.

At present, executive departments and agencies (agencies) employ ad hoc, agency-specific policies, procedures, and markings to safeguard and control this information, such as information that involves privacy, security, proprietary business interests, and law enforcement investigations. This inefficient, confusing patchwork has resulted in inconsistent marking and safeguarding of documents, led to unclear or unnecessarily restrictive dissemination policies, and created impediments to authorized information sharing. The fact that these agency-specific policies are often hidden from public view has only aggravated these issues.

To address these problems, this order establishes a program for managing this information, hereinafter described as Controlled Unclassified Information, that emphasizes the openness and uniformity of Government-wide practice.

Sec. 2. Controlled Unclassified Information (CUI).

(a) The CUI categories and subcategories shall serve as exclusive designations for identifying unclassified information throughout the executive branch that requires safeguarding or dissemination controls, pursuant to and consistent with applicable law, regulations, and Government-wide policies.

(b) The mere fact that information is designated as CUI shall not have a bearing on determinations pursuant to any law requiring the disclosure of information or permitting disclosure as a matter of discretion, including disclosures to the legislative or judicial branches.

(c) The National Archives and Records Administration shall serve as the Executive Agent to implement this order and oversee agency actions to ensure compliance with this order.

Sec. 3. Review of Current Designations.

(a) Each agency head shall, within 180 days of the date of this order:

(1) review all categories, subcategories, and markings used by the agency to designate unclassified information for safeguarding or dissemination controls; and

(2) submit to the Executive Agent a catalogue of proposed categories and subcategories of CUI, and proposed associated markings for information designated as CUI under section 2(a) of this order. This submission shall provide definitions for each proposed category and subcategory and identify the basis in law, regulation, or Government-wide policy for safeguarding or dissemination controls.

(b) If there is significant doubt about whether information should be designated as CUI, it shall not be so designated.

Sec. 4. Development of CUI Categories and Policies.

(a) On the basis of the submissions under section 3 of this order or future proposals, and in consultation with affected agencies, the Executive Agent shall, in a timely manner, approve categories and subcategories of CUI and associated markings to be applied uniformly throughout the executive branch and to become effective upon publication in the registry established under subsection (d) of this section. No unclassified information meeting the requirements of section 2(a) of this order shall be disapproved for inclusion as CUI, but the Executive Agent may resolve conflicts among categories and subcategories of CUI to achieve uniformity and may determine the markings to be used.

(b) The Executive Agent, in consultation with affected agencies, shall develop and issue such directives as are necessary to implement this order. Such directives shall be made available to the public and shall provide policies and procedures concerning marking, safeguarding, dissemination, and decontrol of CUI that, to the extent practicable and permitted by law, regulation, and Government-wide policies, shall remain consistent across categories and subcategories of CUI and throughout the executive branch. In developing such directives, appropriate consideration should be given to the report of the interagency Task Force on Controlled Unclassified Information published in August 2009. The Executive Agent shall issue initial directives for the implementation of this order within 180 days of the date of this order.

(c) The Executive Agent shall convene and chair interagency meetings to discuss matters pertaining to the program established by this order.

(d) Within 1 year of the date of this order, the Executive Agent shall establish and maintain a public CUI registry reflecting authorized CUI categories and subcategories, associated markings, and applicable safeguarding, dissemination, and decontrol procedures.

(e) If the Executive Agent and an agency cannot reach agreement on an issue related to the implementation of this order, that issue may be appealed to the President through the Director of the Office of Management and Budget.

(f) In performing its functions under this order, the Executive Agent, in accordance with applicable law, shall consult with representatives of the public and State, local, tribal, and private sector partners on matters related to approving categories and subcategories of CUI and developing implementing directives issued by the Executive Agent pursuant to this order.

Sec. 5. Implementation.

(a) Within 180 days of the issuance of initial policies and procedures by the Executive Agent in accordance with section 4(b) of this order, each agency that originates or handles CUI shall provide the Executive Agent with a proposed plan for compliance with the requirements of this order, including the establishment of interim target dates.

(b) After a review of agency plans, and in consultation with affected agencies and the Office of Management and Budget, the Executive Agent shall establish deadlines for phased implementation by agencies.

(c) In each of the first 5 years following the date of this order and biennially thereafter, the Executive Agent shall publish a report on the status of agency implementation of this order.

Sec. 6. General Provisions.

(a) This order shall be implemented in a manner consistent with:

(1) applicable law, including protections of confidentiality and privacy rights;

(2) the statutory authority of the heads of agencies, including authorities related to the protection of information provided by the private sector to the Federal Government; and

(3) applicable Government-wide standards and guidelines issued by the National Institute of Standards and Technology, and applicable policies established by the Office of Management and Budget.

(b) The Director of National Intelligence (Director), with respect to the Intelligence Community and after consultation with the heads of affected agencies, may issue such policy directives and guidelines as the Director deems necessary to implement this order with respect to intelligence and intelligence-related information. Procedures or other guidance issued by Intelligence Community element heads shall be in accordance with such policy directives or guidelines issued by the Director. Any such policy directives or guidelines issued by the Director shall be in accordance with this order and directives issued by the Executive Agent.

(c) This order shall not be construed to impair or otherwise affect the functions of the Director of the Office of Management and Budget relating to budgetary, administrative, and legislative proposals.

(d) This order is not intended to, and does not, create any right or benefit, substantive or procedural, enforceable at law or in equity by any party against the United States, its departments, agencies, or entities, its officers, employees, or agents, or any other person.

(e) This order shall be implemented subject to the availability of appropriations.

(f) The Attorney General, upon request by the head of an agency or the Executive Agent, shall render an interpretation of this order with respect to any question arising in the course of its administration.

(g) The Presidential Memorandum of May 7, 2008, entitled "Designation and Sharing of Controlled Unclassified Information (CUI)" is hereby rescinded.

BARACK OBAMA

THE WHITE HOUSE,
November 4, 2010

32 CFR PART 2002 - CONTROLLED UNCLASSIFIED INFORMATION (CUI)

32 CFR PART 2002 - CONTROLLED UNCLASSIFIED INFORMATION (CUI)

Authority: E.O. 13556, 75 FR 68675, 3 CFR, 2010 Comp., pp. 267-270.

Source: 81 FR 63336, Sept. 14, 2016, unless otherwise noted.

Subpart A - General Information

§ 2002.1 Purpose and scope.

(a) This part describes the executive branch's Controlled Unclassified Information (CUI) Program (the CUI Program) and establishes policy for designating, handling, and decontrolling information that qualifies as CUI.

(b) The CUI Program standardizes the way the executive branch handles information that requires protection under laws, regulations, or Government-wide policies, but that does not qualify as classified under Executive Order 13526, Classified National Security Information, December 29, 2009 (3 CFR, 2010 Comp., p. 298), or any predecessor or successor order, or the Atomic Energy Act of 1954 (42 U.S.C. 2011, *et seq.*), as amended.

(c) All unclassified information throughout the executive branch that requires any safeguarding or dissemination control is CUI. Law, regulation (to include this part), or Government-wide policy must require or permit such controls. Agencies therefore may not implement safeguarding or dissemination controls for any unclassified information other than those controls consistent with the CUI Program.

(d) Prior to the CUI Program, agencies often employed *ad hoc,* agency-specific policies, procedures, and markings to handle this information. This patchwork approach caused agencies to mark and handle information inconsistently, implement unclear or unnecessarily restrictive disseminating policies, and create obstacles to sharing information.

(e) An executive branch-wide CUI policy balances the need to safeguard CUI with the public interest in sharing information appropriately and without unnecessary burdens.

(f) This part applies to all executive branch agencies that designate or handle information that meets the standards for CUI. This part does not apply directly to non-executive branch entities, but it does apply indirectly to non-executive branch CUI recipients, through incorporation into agreements (see §§ 2002.4(c) and 2002.16(a) for more information).

(g) This part rescinds Controlled Unclassified Information (CUI) Office Notice 2011-01: Initial Implementation Guidance for Executive Order 13556 (June 9, 2011).

(h) This part creates no right or benefit, substantive or procedural, enforceable by law or in equity by any party against the United States, its departments, agencies, or entities, its officers, employees, or agents, or any other person.

(i) This part, which contains the CUI Executive Agent (EA)'s control policy, overrides agency-specific or *ad hoc* requirements when they conflict. This part does not alter, limit, or supersede a requirement stated in laws, regulations, or Government-wide policies or impede the statutory authority of agency heads.

§ 2002.2 Incorporation by reference.

(a) NARA incorporates certain material by reference into this part with the approval of the Director of the Federal Register under 5 U.S.C. 552(a) and 1 CFR part 51. To enforce any edition other than that specified in this section, NARA must publish notice of change in the Federal Register and the material must be available to the public. You may inspect all approved material incorporated by reference at NARA's textual research room, located at National Archives and Records

Administration; 8601 Adelphi Road; Room 2000; College Park, MD 20740-6001. To arrange to inspect this approved material at NARA, contact NARA's Regulation Comments Desk (Strategy and Performance Division (SP)) by email at *regulation_comments@nara.gov* or by telephone at 301.837.3151. All approved material is available from the sources listed below. You may also inspect approved material at the Office of the Federal Register (OFR). For information on the availability of this material at the OFR, call 202-741-6030 or go to *http://www.archives.gov/federal_register/code_of_federal_regulations/ibr_locations.html*.

(b) The National Institute of Standards and Technology (NIST), by mail at 100 Bureau Drive, Stop 1070; Gaithersburg, MD 20899-1070, by email at *inquiries@nist.gov*, by phone at (301) 975-NIST (6478) or Federal Relay Service (800) 877-8339 (TTY), or online at *http://nist.gov/publication-portal.cfm*.

(1) FIPS PUB 199, Standards for Security Categorization of Federal Information and Information Systems, February 2004. IBR approved for §§ 2002.14(c) and (g), and 2002.16(c).

(2) FIPS PUB 200, Minimum Security Requirements for Federal Information and Information Systems, March 2006. IBR approved for §§ 2002.14(c) and (g), and 2002.16(c).

(3) NIST Special Publication 800-53, Security and Privacy Controls for Federal Information Systems and Organizations, Revision 4, April 2013 (includes updates as of 01-22-2015), (NIST SP 800-53). IBR approved for §§ 2002.14(c), (e), (f), and (g), and 2002.16(c).

(4) NIST Special Publication 800-88, Guidelines for Media Sanitization, Revision 1, December 2014, (NIST SP 800-88). IBR approved for § 2002.14(f).

(5) NIST Special Publication 800-171, Protecting Controlled Unclassified Information in Nonfederal Systems and Organizations, June 2015 (includes updates as of January 14, 2016), (NIST SP 800-171). IBR approved for § 2002.14(h).

§ 2002.4 Definitions.

As used in this part:

(a) ***Agency*** (also Federal agency, executive agency, executive branch agency) is any "executive agency," as defined in 5 U.S.C. 105; the United States Postal Service; and any other independent entity within the executive branch that designates or handles CUI.

(b) ***Agency CUI policies*** are the policies the agency enacts to implement the CUI Program within the agency. They must be in accordance with the Order, this part, and the CUI Registry and approved by the CUI EA.

(c) ***Agreements and arrangements*** are any vehicle that sets out specific CUI handling requirements for contractors and other information-sharing partners when the arrangement with the other party involves CUI. Agreements and arrangements include, but are not limited to, contracts, grants, licenses, certificates, memoranda of agreement/arrangement or understanding, and information-sharing agreements or arrangements. When disseminating or sharing CUI with non-executive branch entities, agencies should enter into written agreements or arrangements that include CUI provisions whenever feasible (see § 2002.16(a)(5) and (6) for details). When sharing information with foreign entities, agencies should enter agreements or arrangements when feasible (see § 2002.16(a)(5)(iii) and (a)(6) for details).

(d) ***Authorized holder*** is an individual, agency, organization, or group of users that is permitted to designate or handle CUI, in accordance with this part.

(e) ***Classified information*** is information that Executive Order 13526, "Classified National Security Information," December 29, 2009 (3 CFR, 2010 Comp., p. 298), or any predecessor or successor order, or the Atomic Energy Act of 1954, as amended, requires agencies to mark with classified markings and protect against unauthorized disclosure.

(f) ***Controlled environment*** is any area or space an authorized holder deems to have adequate physical or procedural controls (*e.g.*, barriers or managed access controls) to protect CUI from unauthorized access or disclosure.

(g) ***Control level*** is a general term that indicates the safeguarding and disseminating requirements associated with CUI Basic and CUI Specified.

(h) ***Controlled Unclassified Information*** (CUI) is information the Government creates or possesses, or that an entity creates or possesses for or on behalf of the Government, that a law, regulation, or Government-wide policy requires or permits an agency to handle using safeguarding or dissemination controls. However, CUI does not include classified information (see paragraph (e) of this section) or information a non-executive branch entity possesses and maintains in its own systems that did not come from, or was not created or possessed by or for, an executive branch agency or an entity acting for an agency. Law, regulation, or Government-wide policy may require or permit safeguarding or dissemination controls in three ways: Requiring or permitting agencies to control or protect the information but providing no specific controls, which makes the information CUI Basic; requiring or permitting agencies to control or protect the information and providing specific controls for doing so, which makes the information CUI Specified; or requiring or permitting agencies to control the information and specifying only some of those controls, which makes the information CUI Specified, but with CUI Basic controls where the authority does not specify.

(i) ***Controls*** are safeguarding or dissemination controls that a law, regulation, or Government-wide policy requires or permits agencies to use when handling CUI. The authority may specify the controls it requires or permits the agency to apply, or the authority may generally require or permit agencies to control the information (in which case, the agency applies controls from the Order, this part, and the CUI Registry).

(j) ***CUI Basic*** is the subset of CUI for which the authorizing law, regulation, or Government-wide policy does not set out specific handling or dissemination controls. Agencies handle CUI Basic according to the uniform set of controls set forth in this part and the CUI Registry. CUI Basic differs from CUI Specified (see definition for CUI Specified in this section), and CUI Basic controls apply whenever CUI Specified ones do not cover the involved CUI.

(k) ***CUI categories and subcategories*** are those types of information for which laws, regulations, or Government-wide policies require or permit agencies to exercise safeguarding or dissemination controls, and which the CUI EA has approved and listed in the CUI Registry. The controls for any CUI Basic categories and any CUI Basic subcategories are the same, but the controls for CUI Specified categories and subcategories can differ from CUI Basic ones and from each other. A CUI category may be Specified, while some or all of its subcategories may not be, and vice versa. If dealing with CUI that falls into a CUI Specified category or subcategory, review the controls for that category or subcategory on the CUI Registry. Also consult the agency's CUI policy for specific direction from the Senior Agency Official.

(l) ***CUI category or subcategory markings*** are the markings approved by the CUI EA for the categories and subcategories listed in the CUI Registry.

(m) ***CUI Executive Agent (EA)*** is the National Archives and Records Administration (NARA), which implements the executive branch-wide CUI Program and oversees Federal agency actions to comply with the Order. NARA has delegated this authority to the Director of the Information Security Oversight Office (ISOO).

(n) ***CUI Program*** is the executive branch-wide program to standardize CUI handling by all Federal agencies. The Program includes the rules, organization, and procedures for CUI, established by the Order, this part, and the CUI Registry.

(o) ***CUI Program manager*** is an agency official, designated by the agency head or CUI SAO, to serve as the official representative to the CUI EA on the agency's day-to-day CUI Program operations, both within the agency and in interagency contexts.

(p) ***CUI Registry*** is the online repository for all information, guidance, policy, and requirements on handling CUI, including everything issued by the CUI EA other than this part. Among other information, the CUI Registry identifies all approved CUI categories and subcategories, provides general descriptions for each, identifies the basis for controls, establishes markings, and includes guidance on handling procedures.

(q) ***CUI senior agency official (SAO)*** is a senior official designated in writing by an agency head and responsible to that agency head for implementation of the CUI Program within that agency. The CUI SAO is the primary point of contact for official correspondence, accountability reporting, and other matters of record between the agency and the CUI EA.

(r) ***CUI Specified*** is the subset of CUI in which the authorizing law, regulation, or Government-wide policy contains specific handling controls that it requires or permits agencies to use that differ from those for CUI Basic. The CUI Registry indicates which laws, regulations, and Government-wide policies include such specific requirements. CUI Specified controls may be more stringent than, or may simply differ from, those required by CUI Basic; the distinction is that the underlying authority spells out specific controls for CUI Specified information and does not for CUI Basic information. CUI Basic controls apply to those aspects of CUI Specified where the authorizing laws, regulations, and Government-wide policies do not provide specific guidance.

(s) ***Decontrolling*** occurs when an authorized holder, consistent with this part and the CUI Registry, removes safeguarding or dissemination controls from CUI that no longer requires such controls. Decontrol may occur automatically or through agency action. See § 2002.18.

(t) ***Designating CUI*** occurs when an authorized holder, consistent with this part and the CUI Registry, determines that a specific item of information falls into a CUI category or subcategory. The authorized holder who designates the CUI must make recipients aware of the information's CUI status in accordance with this part.

(u) ***Designating agency*** is the executive branch agency that designates or approves the designation of a specific item of information as CUI.

(v) ***Disseminating*** occurs when authorized holders provide access, transmit, or transfer CUI to other authorized holders through any means, whether internal or external to an agency.

(w) ***Document*** means any tangible thing which constitutes or contains information, and means the original and any copies (whether different from the originals because of notes made on such copies or otherwise) of all writings of every kind and description over which an agency has authority, whether inscribed by hand or by mechanical, facsimile, electronic, magnetic, microfilm, photographic, or other means, as well as phonic or visual reproductions or oral statements, conversations, or events, and including, but not limited to: Correspondence, email, notes, reports, papers, files, manuals, books, pamphlets, periodicals, letters, memoranda, notations, messages, telegrams, cables, facsimiles, records, studies, working papers, accounting papers, contracts, licenses, certificates, grants, agreements, computer disks, computer tapes, telephone logs, computer mail, computer printouts, worksheets, sent or received communications of any kind, teletype messages, agreements, diary entries, calendars and journals, printouts, drafts, tables, compilations, tabulations, recommendations, accounts, work papers, summaries, address books, other records and recordings or transcriptions of conferences, meetings, visits, interviews, discussions, or telephone conversations, charts, graphs, indexes, tapes, minutes, contracts, leases, invoices, records of purchase or sale correspondence, electronic or other transcription of taping of personal conversations or conferences, and any written, printed, typed, punched, taped, filmed, or graphic matter however produced or reproduced. Document also includes the file, folder, exhibits, and containers, the labels on them, and any metadata, associated with each original or copy. Document also includes voice records, film, tapes, video tapes, email, personal computer files, electronic matter, and other data compilations from which information can be obtained, including materials used in data processing.

(x) ***Federal information system*** is an information system used or operated by an agency or by a contractor of an agency or other organization *on behalf of an agency.* 44 U.S.C. 3554(a)(1)(A)(ii).

(y) ***Foreign entity*** is a foreign government, an international organization of governments or any element thereof, an international or foreign public or judicial body, or an international or foreign private or non-governmental organization.

(z) ***Formerly Restricted Data (FRD)*** is a type of information classified under the Atomic Energy Act, and defined in 10 CFR 1045, Nuclear Classification and Declassification.

(aa) ***Handling*** is any use of CUI, including but not limited to marking, safeguarding, transporting, disseminating, re-using, and disposing of the information.

(bb) ***Lawful Government purpose*** is any activity, mission, function, operation, or endeavor that the U.S. Government authorizes or recognizes as within the scope of its legal authorities or the legal authorities of non-executive branch entities (such as state and local law enforcement).

(cc) ***Legacy material*** is unclassified information that an agency marked as restricted from access or dissemination in some way, or otherwise controlled, prior to the CUI Program.

(dd) ***Limited dissemination control*** is any CUI EA-approved control that agencies may use to limit or specify CUI dissemination.

(ee) ***Misuse of CUI*** occurs when someone uses CUI in a manner not in accordance with the policy contained in the Order, this part, the CUI Registry, agency CUI policy, or the applicable laws, regulations, and Government-wide policies that govern the affected information. This may include intentional violations or unintentional errors in safeguarding or disseminating CUI. This may also include designating or marking information as CUI when it does not qualify as CUI.

(ff) ***National Security System*** is a special type of information system (including telecommunications systems) whose function, operation, or use is defined in National Security Directive 42 and 44 U.S.C. 3542(b)(2).

(gg) ***Non-executive branch entity*** is a person or organization established, operated, and controlled by individual(s) acting outside the scope of any official capacity as officers, employees, or agents of the executive branch of the Federal Government. Such entities may include: Elements of the legislative or judicial branches of the Federal Government; state, interstate, tribal, or local government elements; and private organizations. Non-executive branch entity does not include foreign entities as defined in this part, nor does it include individuals or organizations when they receive CUI information pursuant to federal disclosure laws, including the Freedom of Information Act (FOIA) and the Privacy Act of 1974.

(hh) ***On behalf of an agency*** occurs when a non-executive branch entity uses or operates an information system or maintains or collects information for the purpose of processing, storing, or transmitting Federal information, and those activities are not incidental to providing a service or product to the Government.

(ii) ***Order*** is Executive Order 13556, Controlled Unclassified Information, November 4, 2010 (3 CFR, 2011 Comp., p. 267), or any successor order.

(jj) ***Portion*** is ordinarily a section within a document, and may include subjects, titles, graphics, tables, charts, bullet statements, sub-paragraphs, bullets points, or other sections.

(kk) ***Protection*** includes all controls an agency applies or must apply when handling information that qualifies as CUI.

(ll) ***Public release*** occurs when the agency that originally designated particular information as CUI makes that information available to the public through the agency's official public release processes. Disseminating CUI to non-executive branch entities as authorized does not constitute public release. Releasing information to an individual pursuant to the Privacy Act of 1974 or disclosing it in response to a FOIA request also does not automatically constitute public release, although it may if that agency ties such actions to its official public release processes. Even though an agency may disclose some CUI to a member of the public, the Government must still control that CUI unless the agency publicly releases it through its official public release processes.

(mm) ***Records*** are agency records and Presidential papers or Presidential records (or Vice-Presidential), as those terms are defined in 44 U.S.C. 3301 and 44 U.S.C. 2201 and 2207. Records also include such items created or maintained by a Government contractor, licensee, certificate holder, or grantee that are subject to the sponsoring agency's control under the terms of the entity's agreement with the agency.

(nn) ***Required or permitted (by a law, regulation, or Government-wide policy)*** is the basis by which information may qualify as CUI. If a law, regulation, or Government-wide policy requires that agencies exercise safeguarding or dissemination controls over certain information, or specifically permits agencies the discretion to do so, then that information qualifies as CUI. The term 'specifically permits' in this context can include language such as "is exempt from" applying certain information release or disclosure requirements, "may" release or disclose the information, "may not be required to" release or disclose the information, "is responsible for protecting" the information, and similar specific but indirect, forms of granting the agency discretion regarding safeguarding or dissemination controls. This does not include general agency or agency head authority and discretion to make decisions, risk assessments, or other broad agency authorities, discretions, and powers, regardless of the source. The CUI Registry reflects all appropriate authorizing authorities.

(oo) ***Restricted Data (RD)*** is a type of information classified under the Atomic Energy Act, defined in 10 CFR part 1045, Nuclear Classification and Declassification.

(pp) ***Re-use*** means incorporating, restating, or paraphrasing information from its originally designated form into a newly created document.

(qq) ***Self-inspection*** is an agency's internally managed review and evaluation of its activities to implement the CUI Program.

(rr) ***Unauthorized disclosure*** occurs when an authorized holder of CUI intentionally or unintentionally discloses CUI without a lawful Government purpose, in violation of restrictions imposed by safeguarding or dissemination controls, or contrary to limited dissemination controls.

(ss) ***Uncontrolled unclassified information*** is information that neither the Order nor the authorities governing classified information cover as protected. Although this information is not controlled or classified, agencies must still handle it in accordance with Federal Information Security Modernization Act (FISMA) requirements.

(tt) ***Working papers*** are documents or materials, regardless of form, that an agency or user expects to revise prior to creating a finished product.

§ 2002.6 CUI Executive Agent (EA).

(a) Section 2(c) of the Order designates NARA as the CUI Executive Agent (EA) to implement the Order and to oversee agency efforts to comply with the Order, this part, and the CUI Registry.

(b) NARA has delegated the CUI EA responsibilities to the Director of ISOO. Under this authority, ISOO staff carry out CUI oversight responsibilities and manage the Federal CUI program.

§ 2002.8 Roles and responsibilities.

(a) The CUI EA:

(1) Develops and issues policy, guidance, and other materials, as needed, to implement the Order, the CUI Registry, and this part, and to establish and maintain the CUI Program;

(2) Consults with affected agencies, Government-wide policy bodies, State, local, Tribal, and private sector partners, and representatives of the public on matters pertaining to CUI as needed;

(3) Establishes, convenes, and chairs the CUI Advisory Council (the Council) to address matters pertaining to the CUI Program. The CUI EA consults with affected agencies to develop and document the Council's structure and procedures, and submits the details to OMB for approval;

(4) Reviews and approves agency policies implementing this part to ensure their consistency with the Order, this part, and the CUI Registry;

(5) Reviews, evaluates, and oversees agencies' actions to implement the CUI Program, to ensure compliance with the Order, this part, and the CUI Registry;

(6) Establishes a management and planning framework, including associated deadlines for phased implementation, based on agency compliance plans submitted pursuant to section 5(b) of the Order, and in consultation with affected agencies and OMB;

(7) Approves categories and subcategories of CUI as needed and publishes them in the CUI Registry;

(8) Maintains and updates the CUI Registry as needed;

(9) Prescribes standards, procedures, guidance, and instructions for oversight and agency self-inspection programs, to include performing on-site inspections;

(10) Standardizes forms and procedures to implement the CUI Program;

(11) Considers and resolves, as appropriate, disputes, complaints, and suggestions about the CUI Program from entities in or outside the Government; and

(12) Reports to the President on implementation of the Order and the requirements of this part. This includes publishing a report on the status of agency implementation at least biennially, or more frequently at the discretion of the CUI EA.

(b) Agency heads:

(1) Ensure agency senior leadership support, and make adequate resources available to implement, manage, and comply with the CUI Program as administered by the CUI EA;

(2) Designate a CUI senior agency official (SAO) responsible for oversight of the agency's CUI Program implementation, compliance, and management, and include the official in agency contact listings;

(3) Approve agency policies, as required, to implement the CUI Program; and

(4) Establish and maintain a self-inspection program to ensure the agency complies with the principles and requirements of the Order, this part, and the CUI Registry.

(c) The CUI SAO:

(1) Must be at the Senior Executive Service level or equivalent;

(2) Directs and oversees the agency's CUI Program;

(3) Designates a CUI Program manager;

(4) Ensures the agency has CUI implementing policies and plans, as needed;

(5) Implements an education and training program pursuant to § 2002.30;

(6) Upon request of the CUI EA under section 5(c) of the Order, provides an update of CUI implementation efforts for subsequent reporting;

(7) Submits to the CUI EA any law, regulation, or Government-wide policy not already incorporated into the CUI Registry that the agency proposes to use to designate unclassified information for safeguarding or dissemination controls;

(8) Coordinates with the CUI EA, as appropriate, any proposed law, regulation, or Government-wide policy that would establish, eliminate, or modify a category or subcategory of CUI, or change information controls applicable to CUI;

(9) Establishes processes for handling CUI decontrol requests submitted by authorized holders;

(10) Includes a description of all existing waivers in the annual report to the CUI EA, along with the rationale for each waiver and, where applicable, the alternative steps the agency is taking to ensure sufficient protection of CUI within the agency;

(11) Develops and implements the agency's self-inspection program;

(12) Establishes a mechanism by which authorized holders (both inside and outside the agency) can contact a designated agency representative for instructions when they receive unmarked or improperly marked information the agency designated as CUI;

(13) Establishes a process to accept and manage challenges to CUI status (which may include improper or absent marking);

(14) Establish processes and criteria for reporting and investigating misuse of CUI; and

(15) Follows the requirements for the CUI SAO listed in § 2002.38(e), regarding waivers for CUI.

(d) The Director of National Intelligence: After consulting with the heads of affected agencies and the Director of ISOO, may issue directives to implement this part with respect to the protection of intelligence sources, methods, and activities. Such directives must be in accordance with the Order, this part, and the CUI Registry.

Subpart B - Key Elements of the CUI Program

§ 2002.10 The CUI Registry.

(a) The CUI EA maintains the CUI Registry, which:

(1) Is the authoritative central repository for all guidance, policy, instructions, and information on CUI (other than the Order and this part);

(2) Is publicly accessible;

(3) Includes authorized CUI categories and subcategories, associated markings, applicable decontrolling procedures, and other guidance and policy information; and

(4) Includes citation(s) to laws, regulations, or Government-wide policies that form the basis for each category and subcategory.

(b) Agencies and authorized holders must follow the instructions contained in the CUI Registry in addition to all requirements in the Order and this part.

§ 2002.12 CUI categories and subcategories.

(a) CUI categories and subcategories are the exclusive designations for identifying unclassified information that a law, regulation, or

Government-wide policy requires or permits agencies to handle by means of safeguarding or dissemination controls. All unclassified information throughout the executive branch that requires any kind of safeguarding or dissemination control is CUI. Agencies may not implement safeguarding or dissemination controls for any unclassified information other than those controls permitted by the CUI Program.

(b) Agencies may use only those categories or subcategories approved by the CUI EA and published in the CUI Registry to designate information as CUI.

§ 2002.14 Safeguarding.

(a) ***General safeguarding policy.***

(1) Pursuant to the Order and this part, and in consultation with affected agencies, the CUI EA issues safeguarding standards in this part and, as necessary, in the CUI Registry, updating them as needed. These standards require agencies to safeguard CUI at all times in a manner that minimizes the risk of unauthorized disclosure while allowing timely access by authorized holders.

(2) Safeguarding measures that agencies are authorized or accredited to use for classified information and national security systems are also sufficient for safeguarding CUI in accordance with the organization's management and acceptance of risk.

(3) Agencies may increase CUI Basic's confidentiality impact level above moderate only internally, or by means of agreements with agencies or non-executive branch entities (including agreements for the operation of an information system on behalf of the agencies). Agencies may not otherwise require controls for CUI Basic at a level higher than permitted in the CUI Basic requirements when disseminating the CUI Basic outside the agency.

(4) Authorized holders must comply with policy in the Order, this part, and the CUI Registry, and review any applicable agency CUI policies

for additional instructions. For information designated as CUI Specified, authorized holders must also follow the procedures in the underlying laws, regulations, or Government-wide policies.

(b) ***CUI safeguarding standards.*** Authorized holders must safeguard CUI using one of the following types of standards:

(1) ***CUI Basic.*** CUI Basic is the default set of standards authorized holders must apply to all CUI unless the CUI Registry annotates that CUI as CUI Specified.

(2) ***CUI Specified.***

(i) Authorized holders safeguard CUI Specified in accordance with the requirements of the underlying authorities indicated in the CUI Registry.

(ii) When the laws, regulations, or Government-wide policies governing a specific type of CUI Specified are silent on either a safeguarding or disseminating control, agencies must apply CUI Basic standards to that aspect of the information's controls, unless this results in treatment that does not accord with the CUI Specified authority. In such cases, agencies must apply the CUI Specified standards and may apply limited dissemination controls listed in the CUI Registry to ensure they treat the information in accord with the CUI Specified authority.

(c) ***Protecting CUI under the control of an authorized holder.*** Authorized holders must take reasonable precautions to guard against unauthorized disclosure of CUI. They must include the following measures among the reasonable precautions:

(1) Establish controlled environments in which to protect CUI from unauthorized access or disclosure and make use of those controlled environments;

(2) Reasonably ensure that unauthorized individuals cannot access or observe CUI, or overhear conversations discussing CUI;

(3) Keep CUI under the authorized holder's direct control or protect it with at least one physical barrier, and reasonably ensure that the authorized holder or the physical barrier protects the CUI from unauthorized access or observation when outside a controlled environment; and

(4) Protect the confidentiality of CUI that agencies or authorized holders process, store, or transmit on Federal information systems in accordance with the applicable security requirements and controls established in FIPS PUB 199, FIPS PUB 200, and NIST SP 800-53, (incorporated by reference, see § 2002.2), and paragraph (g) of this section.

(d) ***Protecting CUI when shipping or mailing.*** When sending CUI, authorized holders:

(1) May use the United States Postal Service or any commercial delivery service when they need to transport or deliver CUI to another entity;

(2) Should use in-transit automated tracking and accountability tools when they send CUI;

(3) May use interoffice or interagency mail systems to transport CUI; and

(4) Must mark packages that contain CUI according to marking requirements contained in this part and in guidance published by the CUI EA. See § 2002.20 for more guidance on marking requirements.

(e) ***Reproducing CUI.*** Authorized holders:

(1) May reproduce (*e.g.*, copy, scan, print, electronically duplicate) CUI in furtherance of a lawful Government purpose; and

(2) Must ensure, when reproducing CUI documents on equipment such as printers, copiers, scanners, or fax machines, that the equipment does

not retain data or the agency must otherwise sanitize it in accordance with NIST SP 800-53 (incorporated by reference, see § 2002.2).

(f) ***Destroying CUI.***

(1) Authorized holders may destroy CUI when:

(i) The agency no longer needs the information; and

(ii) Records disposition schedules published or approved by NARA allow.

(2) When destroying CUI, including in electronic form, agencies must do so in a manner that makes it unreadable, indecipherable, and irrecoverable. Agencies must use any destruction method specifically required by law, regulation, or Government-wide policy for that CUI. If the authority does not specify a destruction method, agencies must use one of the following methods:

(i) Guidance for destruction in NIST SP 800-53, Security and Privacy Controls for Federal Information Systems and Organizations, and NIST SP 800-88, Guidelines for Media Sanitization (incorporated by reference, see § 2002.2); or

(ii) Any method of destruction approved for Classified National Security Information, as delineated in 32 CFR 2001.47, Destruction, or any implementing or successor guidance.

(g) ***Information systems that process, store, or transmit CUI.*** In accordance with FIPS PUB 199 (incorporated by reference, see § 2002.2), CUI Basic is categorized at no less than the moderate confidentiality impact level. FIPS PUB 199 defines the security impact levels for Federal information and Federal information systems. Agencies must also apply the appropriate security requirements and controls from FIPS PUB 200 and NIST SP 800-53 (incorporated by reference, see § 2002.2) to CUI in accordance with any risk-based tailoring decisions they make. Agencies may increase CUI Basic's confidentiality impact level above moderate only internally, or by means of agreements with agencies or non-executive branch entities (including agreements for the operation of an information system on behalf of the agencies). Agencies may not otherwise require controls for CUI Basic at a level higher or different from those permitted in the CUI Basic requirements when disseminating the CUI Basic outside the agency.

(h) Information systems that process, store, or transmit CUI are of two different types:

(1) A Federal information system is an information system used or operated by an agency or by a contractor of an agency or other organization on behalf of an agency. An information system operated on behalf of an agency provides information processing services to the agency that the Government might otherwise perform itself but has decided to outsource. This includes systems operated exclusively for Government use and systems operated for multiple users (multiple Federal agencies or Government and private sector users). Information systems that a non-executive branch entity operates on behalf of an agency are subject to the requirements of this part as though they are the agency's systems, and agencies may require these systems to meet additional requirements the agency sets for its own internal systems.

(2) A non-Federal information system is any information system that does not meet the criteria for a Federal information system. Agencies may not treat non-Federal information systems as though they are agency systems, so agencies cannot require that non-executive branch entities protect these systems in the same manner that the agencies might protect their own information systems. When a non-executive branch entity receives Federal information only incidental to providing a service or product to the Government other than processing services, its information systems are not considered Federal information systems. NIST SP 800-171 (incorporated by reference, see § 2002.2) defines the requirements necessary to protect CUI Basic on non-Federal information systems in accordance with the requirements of this part. Agencies must use NIST SP 800-171 when establishing security requirements to protect CUI's confidentiality on non-Federal information systems (unless the authorizing law, regulation, or Government-wide policy listed in the CUI Registry for the CUI

category or subcategory of the information involved prescribes specific safeguarding requirements for protecting the information's confidentiality, or unless an agreement establishes requirements to protect CUI Basic at higher than moderate confidentiality).

§ 2002.16 Accessing and disseminating.

(a) ***General policy*** -

(1) ***Access.*** Agencies should disseminate and permit access to CUI, provided such access or dissemination:

(i) Abides by the laws, regulations, or Government-wide policies that established the CUI category or subcategory;

(ii) Furthers a lawful Government purpose;

(iii) Is not restricted by an authorized limited dissemination control established by the CUI EA; and,

(iv) Is not otherwise prohibited by law.

(2) ***Dissemination controls.***

(i) Agencies must impose dissemination controls judiciously and should do so only to apply necessary restrictions on access to CUI, including those required by law, regulation, or Government-wide policy.

(ii) Agencies may not impose controls that unlawfully or improperly restrict access to CUI.

(3) ***Marking.*** Prior to disseminating CUI, authorized holders must label CUI according to marking guidance issued by the CUI EA, and must include any specific markings required by law, regulation, or Government-wide policy.

(4) ***Reasonable expectation.*** To disseminate CUI to a non-executive branch entity, authorized holders must reasonably expect that all intended recipients are authorized to receive the CUI and have a basic understanding of how to handle it.

(5) ***Agreements.*** Agencies should enter into agreements with any non-executive branch or foreign entity with which the agency shares or intends to share CUI, as follows (except as provided in paragraph (a)(7) of this section):

(i) ***Information-sharing agreements.*** When agencies intend to share CUI with a non-executive branch entity, they should enter into a formal agreement (see § 2004.4(c) for more information on agreements), whenever feasible. Such an agreement may take any form the agency head approves, but when established, it must include a requirement to comply with Executive Order 13556, Controlled Unclassified Information, November 4, 2010 (3 CFR, 2011 Comp., p. 267) or any successor order (the Order), this part, and the CUI Registry.

(ii) ***Sharing CUI without a formal agreement.*** When an agency cannot enter into agreements under paragraph (a)(6)(i) of this section, but the agency's mission requires it to disseminate CUI to non-executive branch entities, the agency must communicate to the recipient that the Government strongly encourages the non-executive branch entity to protect CUI in accordance with the Order, this part, and the CUI Registry, and that such protections should accompany the CUI if the entity disseminates it further.

(iii) ***Foreign entity sharing.*** When entering into agreements or arrangements with a foreign entity, agencies should encourage that entity to protect CUI in accordance with the Order, this part, and the CUI Registry to the extent possible, but agencies may use their judgment as to what and how much to communicate, keeping in mind the ultimate goal of safeguarding CUI. If such agreements or arrangements include safeguarding or dissemination controls on unclassified information, the agency must not establish a parallel protection regime to the CUI Program: For example, the agency must use CUI markings rather than alternative ones (*e.g.,* such as SBU) for safeguarding or dissemination controls on CUI received from or sent to foreign entities, must abide by any requirements set by the CUI category or subcategory's governing laws, regulations, or Government-wide policies, etc.

(iv) ***Pre-existing agreements.*** When an agency entered into an information-sharing agreement prior to November 14, 2016, the agency should modify any terms in that agreement that conflict with the requirements in the Order, this part, and the CUI Registry, when feasible.

(6) ***Agreement content.*** At a minimum, agreements with non-executive branch entities must include provisions that state:

(i) Non-executive branch entities must handle CUI in accordance with the Order, this part, and the CUI Registry;

(ii) Misuse of CUI is subject to penalties established in applicable laws, regulations, or Government-wide policies; and

(iii) The non-executive branch entity must report any non-compliance with handling requirements to the disseminating agency using methods approved by that agency's SAO. When the disseminating agency is not the designating agency, the disseminating agency must notify the designating agency.

(7) ***Exceptions to agreements.*** Agencies need not enter a written agreement when they share CUI with the following entities:

(i) Congress, including any committee, subcommittee, joint committee, joint subcommittee, or office thereof;

(ii) A court of competent jurisdiction, or any individual or entity when directed by an order of a court of competent jurisdiction or a Federal administrative law judge (ALJ) appointed under 5 U.S.C. 3501;

(iii) The Comptroller General, in the course of performing duties of the Government Accountability Office; or

(iv) Individuals or entities, when the agency releases information to them pursuant to a FOIA or Privacy Act request.

(b) ***Controls on accessing and disseminating CUI*** -

(1) ***CUI Basic.*** Authorized holders should disseminate and encourage access to CUI Basic for any recipient when the access meets the requirements set out in paragraph (a)(1) of this section.

(2) ***CUI Specified.*** Authorized holders disseminate and allow access to CUI Specified as required or permitted by the authorizing laws, regulations, or Government-wide policies that established that CUI Specified.

(i) The CUI Registry annotates CUI that requires or permits Specified controls based on law, regulation, and Government-wide policy.

(ii) In the absence of specific dissemination restrictions in the authorizing law, regulation, or Government-wide policy, agencies may disseminate CUI Specified as they would CUI Basic.

(3) ***Receipt of CUI.*** Non-executive branch entities may receive CUI directly from members of the executive branch or as sub-recipients from other non-executive branch entities.

(4) ***Limited dissemination.***

(i) Agencies may place additional limits on disseminating CUI only through use of the limited dissemination controls approved by the CUI EA and published in the CUI Registry. These limited dissemination controls are separate from any controls that a CUI Specified authority requires or permits.

(ii) Using limited dissemination controls to unnecessarily restrict access to CUI is contrary to the goals of the CUI Program. Agencies may therefore use these controls only when it furthers a lawful Government purpose, or laws, regulations, or Government-wide policies require or permit an agency to do so. If an authorized holder has significant doubt about whether it is appropriate to use a limited dissemination control, the authorized holder should consult with and follow the designating agency's policy. If, after consulting the policy, significant doubt still remains, the authorized holder should not apply the limited dissemination control.

(iii) Only the designating agency may apply limited dissemination controls to CUI. Other entities that receive CUI and seek to apply additional controls must request permission to do so from the designating agency.

(iv) Authorized holders may apply limited dissemination controls to any CUI for which they are required or permitted to restrict access by or to certain entities.

(v) Designating entities may combine approved limited dissemination controls listed in the CUI Registry to accommodate necessary practices.

(c) ***Methods of disseminating CUI.***

(1) Before disseminating CUI, authorized holders must reasonably expect that all intended recipients have a lawful Government purpose to receive the CUI. Authorized holders may then disseminate the CUI by any method that meets the safeguarding requirements of this part and the CUI Registry and ensures receipt in a timely manner, unless the laws, regulations, or Government-wide policies that govern that CUI require otherwise.

(2) To disseminate CUI using systems or components that are subject to NIST guidelines and publications (*e.g.*, email applications, text messaging, facsimile, or voicemail), agencies must do so in accordance with the no-less-than-moderate confidentiality impact

value set out in FIPS PUB 199, FIPS PUB 200, NIST SP 800-53 (incorporated by reference, see § 2002.2).

§ 2002.18 Decontrolling.

(a) Agencies should decontrol as soon as practicable any CUI designated by their agency that no longer requires safeguarding or dissemination controls, unless doing so conflicts with the governing law, regulation, or Government-wide policy.

(b) Agencies may decontrol CUI automatically upon the occurrence of one of the conditions below, or through an affirmative decision by the designating agency:

(1) When laws, regulations or Government-wide policies no longer require its control as CUI and the authorized holder has the appropriate authority under the authorizing law, regulation, or Government-wide policy;

(2) When the designating agency decides to release it to the public by making an affirmative, proactive disclosure;

(3) When the agency discloses it in accordance with an applicable information access statute, such as the FOIA, or the Privacy Act (when legally permissible), if the agency incorporates such disclosures into its public release processes; or

(4) When a pre-determined event or date occurs, as described in § 2002.20(g), unless law, regulation, or Government-wide policy requires coordination first.

(c) The designating agency may also decontrol CUI:

(1) In response to a request by an authorized holder to decontrol it; or

(2) Concurrently with any declassification action under Executive Order 13526 or any predecessor or successor order, as long as the information also appropriately qualifies for decontrol as CUI.

(d) An agency may designate in its CUI policies which agency personnel it authorizes to decontrol CUI, consistent with law, regulation, and Government-wide policy.

(e) Decontrolling CUI relieves authorized holders from requirements to handle the information under the CUI Program, but does not constitute authorization for public release.

(f) Authorized holders must clearly indicate that CUI is no longer controlled when restating, paraphrasing, re-using, releasing to the public, or donating it to a private institution. Otherwise, authorized holders do not have to mark, review, or take other actions to indicate the CUI is no longer controlled.

(1) Agency policy may allow authorized holders to remove or strike through only those CUI markings on the first or cover page of the decontrolled CUI and markings on the first page of any attachments that contain CUI.

(2) If an authorized holder uses the decontrolled CUI in a newly created document, the authorized holder must remove all CUI markings for the decontrolled information.

(g) Once decontrolled, any public release of information that was formerly CUI must be in accordance with applicable law and agency policies on the public release of information.

(h) Authorized holders may request that the designating agency decontrol certain CUI.

(i) If an authorized holder publicly releases CUI in accordance with the designating agency's authorized procedures, the release constitutes decontrol of the information.

(j) Unauthorized disclosure of CUI does not constitute decontrol.

(k) Agencies must not decontrol CUI in an attempt to conceal, or to otherwise circumvent accountability for, an identified unauthorized disclosure.

(l) When laws, regulations, or Government-wide policies require specific decontrol procedures, authorized holders must follow such requirements.

(m) The Archivist of the United States may decontrol records transferred to the National Archives in accordance with § 2002.34, absent a specific agreement otherwise with the designating agency. The Archivist decontrols records to facilitate public access pursuant to 44 U.S.C. 2108 and NARA's regulations at 36 CFR parts 1235, 1250, and 1256.

§ 2002.20 Marking.

(a) ***General marking policy.***

(1) CUI markings listed in the CUI Registry are the only markings authorized to designate unclassified information requiring safeguarding or dissemination controls. Agencies and authorized holders must, in accordance with the implementation timelines established for the agency by the CUI EA:

(i) Discontinue all use of legacy or other markings not permitted by this part or included in the CUI Registry; and

(ii) Uniformly and conspicuously apply CUI markings to all CUI exclusively in accordance with the part and the CUI Registry, unless this part or the CUI EA otherwise specifically permits. See paragraph (a)(6) of this section and §§ 2002.38, Waivers of CUI requirements, and 2002.36, Legacy materials, for more information.

(2) Agencies may not modify CUI Program markings or deviate from the method of use prescribed by the CUI EA (in this part and the CUI

Registry) in an effort to accommodate existing agency marking practices, except in circumstances approved by the CUI EA. The CUI Program prohibits using markings or practices not included in this part or the CUI Registry. If legacy markings remain on information, the legacy markings are void and no longer indicate that the information is protected or that it is or qualifies as CUI.

(3) An agency receiving an incorrectly marked document should notify either the disseminating entity or the designating agency, and request a properly marked document.

(4) The designating agency determines that the information qualifies for CUI status and applies the appropriate CUI marking when it designates that information as CUI.

(5) If an agency has information within its control that qualifies as CUI but has not been previously marked as CUI for any reason (for example, pursuant to an agency internal marking waiver as referenced in § 2002.38 (a)), the agency must mark it as CUI prior to disseminating it.

(6) Agencies must not mark information as CUI to conceal illegality, negligence, ineptitude, or other disreputable circumstances embarrassing to any person, any agency, the Federal Government, or any of their partners, or for any purpose other than to adhere to the law, regulation, or Government-wide policy authorizing the control.

(7) The lack of a CUI marking on information that qualifies as CUI does not exempt the authorized holder from abiding by applicable handling requirements as described in the Order, this part, and the CUI Registry.

(8) When it is impractical for an agency to individually mark CUI due to quantity or nature of the information, or when an agency has issued a limited CUI marking waiver, authorized holders must make recipients aware of the information's CUI status using an alternate marking method that is readily apparent (for example, through user access agreements, a computer system digital splash screen (*e.g.,* alerts

that flash up when accessing the system), or signs in storage areas or on containers).

(b) ***The CUI banner marking.*** Designators of CUI must mark all CUI with a CUI banner marking, which may include up to three elements:

(1) ***The CUI control marking (mandatory).***

(i) The CUI control marking may consist of either the word "CONTROLLED" or the acronym "CUI," at the designator's discretion. Agencies may specify in their CUI policy that employees must use one or the other.

(ii) The CUI Registry contains additional, specific guidance and instructions for using the CUI control marking.

(iii) Authorized holders who designate CUI may not use alternative markings to identify or mark items as CUI.

(2) ***CUI category or subcategory markings (mandatory for CUI Specified).***

(i) The CUI Registry lists the category and subcategory markings, which align with the CUI's governing category or subcategory.

(ii) Although the CUI Program does not require agencies to use category or subcategory markings on CUI Basic, an agency's CUI SAO may establish agency policy that mandates use of CUI category or subcategory markings on CUI Basic.

(iii) However, authorized holders must include in the CUI banner marking all CUI Specified category or subcategory markings that pertain to the information in the document. If law, regulation, or Government-wide policy requires specific marking, disseminating, informing, distribution limitation, or warning statements, agencies must use those indicators as those authorities require or permit. However, agencies must not include these additional indicators in the CUI banner marking or CUI portion markings.

(iv) The CUI Registry contains additional, specific guidance and instructions for using CUI category and subcategory markings.

(3) ***Limited dissemination control markings.***

(i) CUI limited dissemination control markings align with limited dissemination controls established by the CUI EA under § 2002.16(b)(4).

(ii) Agency policy should include specific criteria establishing which authorized holders may apply limited dissemination controls and their corresponding markings, and when. Such agency policy must align with the requirements in § 2002.16(b)(4).

(iii) The CUI Registry contains additional, specific guidance and instructions for using limited dissemination control markings.

(c) ***Using the CUI banner marking.***

(1) The content of the CUI banner marking must apply to the whole document (*i.e.,* inclusive of all CUI within the document) and must be the same on each page of the document that includes CUI.

(2) The CUI Registry contains additional, specific guidelines and instructions for using the CUI banner marking.

(d) ***CUI designation indicator (mandatory).***

(1) All documents containing CUI must carry an indicator of who designated the CUI within it. This must include the designator's agency (at a minimum) and may take any form that identifies the designating agency, including letterhead or other standard agency indicators, or adding a "Controlled by" line (for example, "Controlled by: Division 5, Department of Good Works.").

(2) The designation indicator must be readily apparent to authorized holders and may appear only on the first page or cover. The CUI

Registry contains additional, specific guidance and requirements for using CUI designation indicators.

(e) ***CUI decontrolling indicators.***

(1) Where feasible, designating agencies must include a specific decontrolling date or event with all CUI. Agencies may do so in any manner that makes the decontrolling schedule readily apparent to an authorized holder.

(2) Authorized holders may consider specific items of CUI as decontrolled as of the date indicated, requiring no further review by, or communication with, the designator.

(3) If using a specific event after which the CUI is considered decontrolled:

(i) The event must be foreseeable and verifiable by any authorized holder (*e.g.,* not based on or requiring special access or knowledge); and

(ii) The designator should include point of contact and preferred method of contact information in the decontrol indicator when using this method, to allow authorized holders to verify that a specified event has occurred.

(4) The CUI Registry contains additional, specific guidance and instructions for using limited dissemination control markings.

(f) ***Portion marking CUI.***

(1) Agencies are permitted and encouraged to portion mark all CUI, to facilitate information sharing and proper handling.

(2) Authorized holders who designate CUI may mark CUI only with portion markings approved by the CUI EA and listed in the CUI Registry.

(3) CUI portion markings consist of the following elements:

(i) The CUI control marking, which must be the acronym "CUI";

(ii) CUI category/subcategory portion markings (if required or permitted); and

(iii) CUI limited dissemination control portion markings (if required).

(4) When using portion markings:

(i) CUI category and subcategory portion markings are optional for CUI Basic. Agencies may manage their use by means of agency policy.

(ii) Authorized holders permitted to designate CUI must portion mark both CUI and uncontrolled unclassified portions.

(5) In cases where portions consist of several segments, such as paragraphs, sub-paragraphs, bullets, and sub-bullets, and the control level is the same throughout, designators of CUI may place a single portion marking at the beginning of the primary paragraph or bullet. However, if the portion includes different CUI categories or subcategories, or if the portion includes some CUI and some uncontrolled unclassified information, authorized holders should portion mark all segments separately to avoid improper control of any one segment.

(6) Each portion must reflect the control level of only that individual portion. If the information contained in a sub-paragraph or sub-bullet is a different CUI category or subcategory from its parent paragraph or parent bullet, this does not make the parent paragraph or parent bullet controlled at that same level.

(7) The CUI Registry contains additional, specific guidance and instructions for using CUI portion markings and uncontrolled unclassified portion markings.

(g) ***Commingling CUI markings with Classified National Security Information (CNSI).*** When authorized holders include CUI in documents that also contain CNSI, the decontrolling provisions of the Order and this part apply only to portions marked as CUI. In addition, authorized holders must:

(1) Portion mark all CUI to ensure that authorized holders can distinguish CUI portions from portions containing classified and uncontrolled unclassified information;

(2) Include the CUI control marking, CUI Specified category and subcategory markings, and limited dissemination control markings in an overall banner marking; and

(3) Follow the requirements of the Order and this part, and instructions in the CUI Registry on marking CUI when commingled with CNSI.

(h) ***Commingling restricted data (RD) and formerly restricted data (FRD) with CUI.***

(1) To the extent possible, avoid commingling RD or FRD with CUI in the same document. When it is not practicable to avoid such commingling, follow the marking requirements in the Order and this part, and instructions in the CUI Registry, as well as the marking requirements in 10 CFR part 1045, Nuclear Classification and Declassification.

(2) Follow the requirements of 10 CFR part 1045 when extracting an RD or FRD portion for use in a new document.

(3) Follow the requirements of the Order and this part, and instructions in the CUI Registry if extracting a CUI portion for use in a new document.

(4) The lack of declassification instructions for RD or FRD portions does not eliminate the requirement to process commingled documents for declassification in accordance with the Atomic Energy Act, or 10 CFR part 1045.

(i) ***Packages and parcels containing CUI.***

(1) Address packages that contain CUI for delivery only to a specific recipient.

(2) Do not put CUI markings on the outside of an envelope or package, or otherwise indicate on the outside that the item contains CUI.

(j) ***Transmittal document marking requirements.***

(1) When a transmittal document accompanies CUI, the transmittal document must include a CUI marking on its face ("CONTROLLED" or "CUI"), indicating that CUI is attached or enclosed.

(2) The transmittal document must also include conspicuously on its face the following or similar instructions, as appropriate:

(i) "When enclosure is removed, this document is Uncontrolled Unclassified Information"; or

(ii) "When enclosure is removed, this document is (control level); upon removal, this document does not contain CUI."

(k) ***Working papers.*** Mark working papers containing CUI the same way as the finished product containing CUI would be marked and as required for any CUI contained within them. Handle them in accordance with this part and the CUI Registry.

(l) ***Using supplemental administrative markings with CUI.***

(1) Agency heads may authorize the use of supplemental administrative markings (*e.g.* "Pre-decisional," "Deliberative," "Draft") for use with CUI.

(2) Agency heads may not authorize the use of supplemental administrative markings to establish safeguarding requirements or disseminating restrictions, or to designate the information as CUI. However, agencies may use these markings to inform recipients of the

non-final status of documents under development to avoid confusion and maintain the integrity of an agency's decision-making process.

(3) Agencies must detail requirements for using supplemental administrative markings with CUI in agency policy that is available to anyone who may come into possession of CUI with these markings.

(4) Authorized holders must not incorporate or include supplemental administrative markings in the CUI marking scheme detailed in this part and the CUI Registry.

(5) Supplemental administrative markings must not duplicate any CUI marking described in this part or the CUI Registry.

(m) ***Unmarked CUI.*** Treat unmarked information that qualifies as CUI as described in the Order, § 2002.8(c), and the CUI Registry.

§ 2002.22 Limitations on applicability of agency CUI policies.

(a) Agency CUI policies do not apply to entities outside that agency unless a law, regulation, or Government-wide policy requires or permits the controls contained in the agency policy to do so, and the CUI Registry lists that law, regulation, or Government-wide policy as a CUI authority.

(b) Agencies may not include additional requirements or restrictions on handling CUI other than those permitted in the Order, this part, or the CUI Registry when entering into agreements.

§ 2002.24 Agency self-inspection program.

(a) The agency must establish a self-inspection program pursuant to the requirement in § 2002.8(b)(4).

(b) The self-inspection program must include:

(1) At least annual review and assessment of the agency's CUI program. The agency head or CUI SAO should determine any greater frequency based on program needs and the degree to which the agency engages in designating CUI;

(2) Self-inspection methods, reviews, and assessments that serve to evaluate program effectiveness, measure the level of compliance, and monitor the progress of CUI implementation;

(3) Formats for documenting self-inspections and recording findings when not prescribed by the CUI EA;

(4) Procedures by which to integrate lessons learned and best practices arising from reviews and assessments into operational policies, procedures, and training;

(5) A process for resolving deficiencies and taking corrective actions; and

(6) Analysis and conclusions from the self-inspection program, documented on an annual basis and as requested by the CUI EA.

Subpart C - CUI Program Management

§ 2002.30 Education and training.

(a) The CUI SAO must establish and implement an agency training policy. At a minimum, the training policy must address the means, methods, and frequency of agency CUI training.

(b) Agency training policy must ensure that personnel who have access to CUI receive training on designating CUI, relevant CUI categories and subcategories, the CUI Registry, associated markings, and applicable safeguarding, disseminating, and decontrolling policies and procedures.

(c) Agencies must train employees on these matters when the employees first begin working for the agency and at least once every two years thereafter.

(d) The CUI EA reviews agency training materials to ensure consistency and compliance with the Order, this part, and the CUI Registry.

§ 2002.32 CUI cover sheets.

(a) Agencies may use cover sheets for CUI. If an agency chooses to use cover sheets, it must use CUI EA-approved cover sheets, which agencies can find on the CUI Registry.

(b) Agencies may use cover sheets to identify CUI, alert observers that CUI is present from a distance, and serve as a shield to protect the attached CUI from inadvertent disclosure.

§ 2002.34 Transferring records.

(a) When feasible, agencies must decontrol records containing CUI prior to transferring them to NARA.

(b) When an agency cannot decontrol records before transferring them to NARA, the agency must:

(1) Indicate on a Transfer Request (TR) in NARA's Electronic Records Archives (ERA) or on an SF 258 paper transfer form, that the records should continue to be controlled as CUI (subject to NARA's regulations on transfer, public availability, and access; see 36 CFR parts 1235, 1250, and 1256); and

(2) For hard copy transfer, do not place a CUI marking on the outside of the container.

(c) If the agency does not indicate the status as CUI on the TR or SF 258, NARA may assume the agency decontrolled the information prior to transfer, regardless of any CUI markings on the actual records.

§ 2002.36 Legacy materials.

(a) Agencies must review documents created prior to November 14, 2016 and re-mark any that contain information that qualifies as CUI in accordance with the Order, this part, and the CUI Registry. When agencies do not individually re-mark legacy material that qualifies as CUI, agencies must use an alternate permitted marking method (see § 2002.20(a)(8)).

(b) When the CUI SAO deems re-marking legacy documents to be excessively burdensome, the CUI SAO may grant a legacy material marking waiver under § 2002.38(b).

(c) When the agency re-uses any information from legacy documents that qualifies as CUI, whether the documents have obsolete control markings or not, the agency must designate the newly-created document (or other re-use) as CUI and mark it accordingly.

§ 2002.38 Waivers of CUI requirements.

(a) ***Limited CUI marking waivers within the agency.*** When an agency designates information as CUI but determines that marking it as CUI is excessively burdensome, an agency's CUI SAO may approve waivers of all or some of the CUI marking requirements while that CUI remains within agency control.

(b) ***Limited legacy material marking waivers within the agency.***

(1) In situations in which the agency has a substantial amount of stored information with legacy markings, and removing legacy markings and designating or re-marking it as CUI would be excessively burdensome,

the agency's CUI SAO may approve a waiver of these requirements for some or all of that information while it remains under agency control.

(2) When an authorized holder re-uses any legacy information or information derived from legacy documents that qualifies as CUI, they must remove or redact legacy markings and designate or re-mark the information as CUI, even if the information is under a legacy material marking waiver prior to re-use.

(c) ***Exigent circumstances waivers.***

(1) In exigent circumstances, the agency head or the CUI SAO may waive the provisions and requirements established in this part or the CUI Registry for any CUI while it is within the agency's possession or control, unless specifically prohibited by applicable laws, regulations, or Government-wide policies.

(2) Exigent circumstances waivers may apply when an agency shares the information with other agencies or non-Federal entities. In such cases, the authorized holders must make recipients aware of the CUI status of any disseminated information.

(d) ***For all waivers.***

(1) The CUI SAO must still ensure that the agency appropriately safeguards and disseminates the CUI. See § 2002.20(a)(7);

(2) The CUI SAO must detail in each waiver the alternate protection methods the agency will employ to ensure protection of CUI subject to the waiver;

(3) All marking waivers apply to CUI subject to the waiver only while that agency continues to possess that CUI. No marking waiver may accompany CUI when an authorized holder disseminates it outside that agency;

(4) Authorized holders must uniformly and conspicuously apply CUI markings to all CUI prior to disseminating it outside the agency unless otherwise specifically permitted by the CUI EA; and

(5) When the circumstances requiring the waiver end, the CUI SAO must reinstitute the requirements for all CUI subject to the waiver without delay.

(e) The CUI SAO must:

(1) Retain a record of each waiver;

(2) Include a description of all current waivers and waivers issued during the preceding year in the annual report to the CUI EA, along with the rationale for each waiver and the alternate steps the agency takes to ensure sufficient protection of CUI; and

(3) Notify authorized recipients and the public of these waivers.

§ 2002.44 CUI and disclosure statutes.

(a) ***General policy.*** The fact that an agency designates certain information as CUI does not affect an agency's or employee's determinations pursuant to any law that requires the agency or the employee to disclose that information or permits them to do so as a matter of discretion. The agency or employee must make such determinations according to the criteria set out in the governing law, not on the basis of the information's status as CUI.

(b) ***CUI and the Freedom of Information Act (FOIA).*** Agencies must not cite the FOIA as a CUI safeguarding or disseminating control authority for CUI. When an agency is determining whether to disclose information in response to a FOIA request, the agency must base its decision on the content of the information and applicability of any FOIA statutory exemptions, regardless of whether an agency designates or marks the information as CUI. There may be circumstances in which an agency may disclose CUI to an individual or entity, including through a

FOIA response, but such disclosure does not always constitute public release as defined in this part. Although disclosed via a FOIA response, the agency may still need to control the CUI while the agency continues to hold the information, despite the disclosure, unless the agency otherwise decontrols it (or the agency includes in its policies that FOIA disclosure always results in public release and the CUI does not otherwise have another legal requirement for its continued control).

(c) ***CUI and the Whistleblower Protection Act.*** This part does not change or affect existing legal protections for whistleblowers. The fact that an agency designates or marks certain information as CUI does not determine whether an individual may lawfully disclose that information under a law or other authority, and does not preempt or otherwise affect whistleblower legal protections provided by law, regulation, or executive order or directive.

§ 2002.46 CUI and the Privacy Act.

The fact that records are subject to the Privacy Act of 1974 does not mean that agencies must mark them as CUI. Consult agency policies or guidance to determine which records may be subject to the Privacy Act; consult the CUI Registry to determine which privacy information must be marked as CUI. Information contained in Privacy Act systems of records may also be subject to controls under other CUI categories or subcategories and the agency may need to mark that information as CUI for that reason. In addition, when determining whether the agency must protect certain information under the Privacy Act, or whether the Privacy Act allows the agency to release the information to an individual, the agency must base its decision on the content of the information and the Privacy Act's criteria, regardless of whether an agency designates or marks the information as CUI.

§ 2002.48 CUI and the Administrative Procedure Act (APA).

Nothing in the regulations in this part alters the Administrative Procedure Act (APA) or the powers of Federal administrative law judges (ALJs) appointed thereunder, including the power to determine confidentiality of information in proceedings over which they preside. Nor do the regulations in this part impose requirements concerning the manner in which ALJs designate, disseminate, control access to, decontrol, or mark such information, or make such determinations.

§ 2002.50 Challenges to designation of information as CUI.

(a) Authorized holders of CUI who, in good faith, believe that its designation as CUI is improper or incorrect, or who believe they have received unmarked CUI, should notify the disseminating agency of this belief. When the disseminating agency is not the designating agency, the disseminating agency must notify the designating agency.

(b) If the information at issue is involved in Government litigation, or the challenge to its designation or marking as CUI arises as part of the litigation, the issue of whether the challenger may access the information will be addressed via the litigation process instead of by the agency CUI program. Challengers should nonetheless notify the agency of the issue through the agency process described below, and include its litigation connection.

(c) CUI SAOs must create a process within their agency to accept and manage challenges to CUI status. At a minimum, this process must include a timely response to the challenger that:

(1) Acknowledges receipt of the challenge;

(2) States an expected timetable for response to the challenger;

(3) Provides an opportunity for the challenger to define a rationale for belief that the CUI in question is inappropriately designated;

(4) Gives contact information for the official making the agency's decision in this matter; and

(5) Ensures that challengers who are authorized holders have the option of bringing such challenges anonymously, and that challengers are not subject to retribution for bringing such challenges.

(d) Until the challenge is resolved, authorized holders should continue to safeguard and disseminate the challenged CUI at the control level indicated in the markings.

(e) If a challenging party disagrees with the response to a challenge, that party may use the Dispute Resolution procedures described in § 2002.52.

§ 2002.52 Dispute resolution for agencies.

(a) When laws, regulations, or Government-wide policies governing the CUI involved in a dispute set out specific procedures, processes, and requirements for resolving disputes, agencies must follow those processes for that CUI. This includes submitting the dispute to someone other than the CUI EA for resolution if the authority so requires. If the CUI at issue is involved in litigation, the agency should refer the issue to the appropriate attorneys for resolution through the litigation process.

(b) When laws, regulations, and Government-wide policies governing the CUI do not set out specific procedures, processes, or requirements for CUI dispute resolution (or the information is not involved in litigation), this part governs.

(c) All parties to a dispute arising from implementing or interpreting the Order, this part, or the CUI Registry should make every effort to resolve the dispute expeditiously. Parties should address disputes within a reasonable, mutually acceptable time period, taking into consideration the parties' mission, sharing, and protection requirements.

(d) If parties to a dispute cannot reach a mutually acceptable resolution, either party may refer the matter to the CUI EA.

(e) The CUI EA acts as the impartial arbiter of the dispute and has the authority to render a decision on the dispute after consulting with all affected parties. If a party to the dispute is also a member of the Intelligence Community, the CUI EA must consult with the Office of the Director of National Intelligence when the CUI EA receives the dispute for resolution.

(f) Until the dispute is resolved, authorized holders should continue to safeguard and disseminate any disputed CUI at the control level indicated in the markings, or as directed by the CUI EA if the information is unmarked.

(g) Parties may appeal the CUI EA's decision through the Director of OMB to the President for resolution, pursuant to section 4(e) of the Order. If one of the parties to the dispute is the CUI EA and the parties cannot resolve the dispute under paragraph (c) of this section, the parties may likewise refer the matter to OMB for resolution.

§ 2002.54 Misuse of CUI.

(a) The CUI SAO must establish agency processes and criteria for reporting and investigating misuse of CUI.

(b) The CUI EA reports findings on any incident involving misuse of CUI to the offending agency's CUI SAO or CUI Program manager for action, as appropriate.

§ 2002.56 Sanctions for misuse of CUI.

(a) To the extent that agency heads are otherwise authorized to take administrative action against agency personnel who misuse CUI, agency CUI policy governing misuse should reflect that authority.

(b) Where laws, regulations, or Government-wide policies governing certain categories or subcategories of CUI specifically establish sanctions, agencies must adhere to such sanctions.

Appendix A to Part 2002 - Acronyms

CNSI - Classified National Security Information

Council or the Council - The CUI Advisory Council

CUI - Controlled unclassified information

EA - The CUI Executive Agent (which is ISOO)

FOIA - Freedom of Information Act

FRD - Formerly Restricted Data

ISOO - Information Security Oversight Office at the National Archives and Records Administration

NARA - National Archives and Records Administration

OMB - Office of Management and Budget within the Office of Information and Regulatory Affairs of the Executive Office of the President

PM - the agency's CUI program manager

RD - Restricted Data

SAO - the senior agency official [for CUI]

TR - Transfer Request in NARA's Electronic Records Archives (ERA)

Marking Controlled Unclassified Information

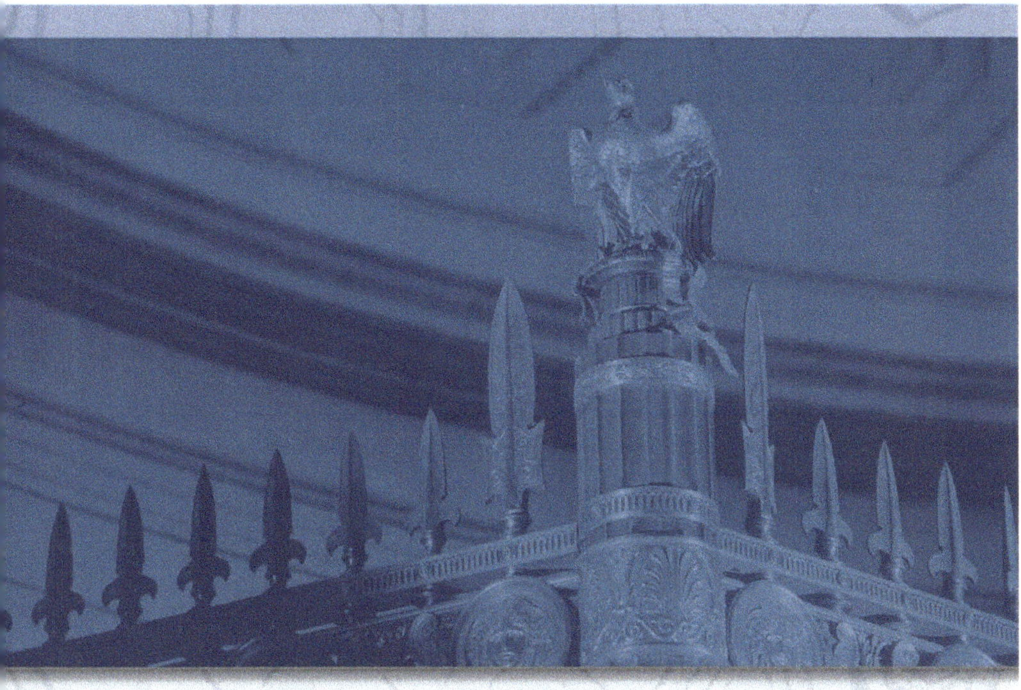

Marking

CUI HANDBOOK 2016-12-06: This guidance document does not have the force and effect of law and is not meant to bind the public, except as authorized by law or regulation or as incorporated into a contract. Accordingly, with regard to the public, this document only provides clarity regarding existing requirements under the law or agency policies. This guidance document is binding on agency actions as authorized under applicable statute, executive order, regulation, or similar authority.

Version 1.1 – December 6, 2016

As required by Executive Order 13556, Controlled Unclassified Information, November 4, 2010, and 32 CFR Part 2002, Controlled Unclassified Information, effective November 14, 2016.

Table of Contents

Table of Contents (con't.)

Introduction

The CUI Program standardizes the way the Executive branch handles unclassified information that does not meet the criteria required for classification under E.O. 13526, "Classified National Security Information," December 29, 2009, or the Atomic Energy Act but must be protected based on law, regulation, or Government-wide policy. That protection involves the safeguards employed while being stored or handled by the Executive branch departments or agencies (hereafter referred to as agencies), as well as the controls involving how the information is disseminated.

Prior to implementation of the CUI Program, agencies employed ad hoc, agency-specific policies, procedures, and markings to safeguard and control this information, such as information that involves privacy, security, proprietary business interests, and law enforcement investigations. This inefficient, confusing patchwork resulted in inconsistent marking and safeguarding of documents, led to unclear or unnecessarily restrictive dissemination policies, and created impediments to authorized information sharing.

This handbook was developed to assist authorized holders by providing examples of correctly marked Controlled Unclassified Information (CUI). Markings alert holders to the presence of CUI and, when portion markings are used, identify the exact information or portion that needs protection. Markings can alert holders to any CUI dissemination and safeguarding controls. While every marking situation is not reflected, this handbook provides basic marking guidelines for CUI, regardless of form.

Employees must review their agency's CUI policy prior to marking any CUI. The handling of CUI must be in accordance with E.O. 13556, "Controlled Unclassified Information," November 4, 2010, (hereafter referred to as the Order), 32 CFR Part 2002, supplemental guidance published by the CUI Executive Agent (EA), and all applicable EA-approved agency policy. This handbook contains guidance on what each marking is, where and how to apply it, and which items are mandatory or optional (based on internal agency policy).

All markings used are for illustration purposes only. This booklet does not contain CUI and may be reproduced without permission.

PART ONE:
CUI MARKINGS IN AN UNCLASSIFIED ENVIRONMENT

The CUI Banner Marking

The CUI Banner Marking:

- The primary marking for all CUI is the CUI Banner Marking. This is the main marking that appears at the top of each page of any document that contains CUI.
- This marking is MANDATORY for all documents containing CUI.
    - The content of the CUI Banner Marking must be inclusive of all CUI within the document and must be the same on each page.
    - The Banner Marking should appear as bold capitalized black text and be centered when feasible.
- The CUI Banner Marking may include up to three elements:
    - The CUI Control Marking (mandatory) may consist of either the word "CONTROLLED" or the acronym "CUI."
    - CUI Category or Subcategory Markings (mandatory for CUI Specified). These are separated from the CUI Control Marking by a double forward slash (//). When including multiple categories or subcategories in a Banner Marking, they must be alphabetized and are separated by a single forward slash (/).
    - Limited Dissemination Control Markings. These are preceded by a double forward slash (//) to separate them from the rest of the CUI Banner Marking.

- Here is a sample of the CUI Banner Marking:

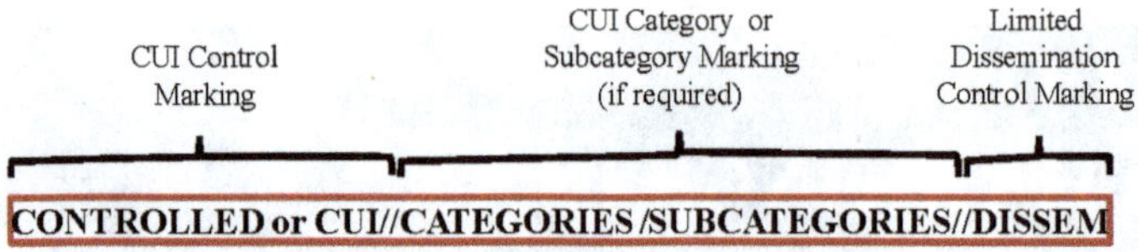

NOTE: The above example uses the words "CATEGORIES" and "SUBCATEGORIES" as substitutes for CUI Category or Subcategory Markings and the word "DISSEM" as a substitute for a Limited Dissemination Control Marking. Consult the CUI Registry for actual CUI markings.

Reference: 32 CFR 2002.20(b) 6

CUI Banner Markings (CUI Control Marking)

The CUI Control Marking is mandatory for all CUI and may consist of either the word "CONTROLLED" or the acronym "CUI" (at the designator's discretion).

As an optional best practice, the CUI Banner Marking may be placed at the bottom of the document as well.

Below are two examples showing the options for the CUI Banner Marking.

MANDATORY:
CUI Banner Markings must appear on the top portion of the page.

CONTROLLED

Department of Good Works
Washington, D.C. 20006

August 27, 2016

MEMORANDUM FOR THE DIRECTOR

From: Elliott Alderson, Chief
Robotics Division

Subject: Examples

We support President Walken by ensuring that the Government protects and provides proper access to information to advance the national and public interest.

We lead efforts to standardize and assess the management of classified and controlled unclassified information through oversight, policy development, guidance, education, and reporting.

CONTROLLED

CUI

Department of Good Works
Washington, D.C. 20006

August 27, 2016

MEMORANDUM FOR THE DIRECTOR

From: Tyrell Wellick
Office of the CTO

Subject: Examples

We support President Walken by ensuring that the Government protects and provides proper access to information to advance the national and public interest.

We lead efforts to standardize and assess the management of classified and controlled unclassified information through oversight, policy development, guidance, education, and reporting.

CUI

Optional Best Practice: Also Placed Centered at Bottom

Reference: 32 CFR 2002.20(b)(1)

CUI Categories and Subcategories

A Bit About CUI Categories and Subcategories:

The CUI Program is founded on the prerequisite that only information requiring protection based in a law, Federal regulation, or government-wide policy can qualify as CUI.

CUI Categories and Subcategories are essentially the different "flavors" of CUI. Each Category and Subcategory is based in at least one (and sometimes many) of these laws, regulations, or government-wide policies – also referred to as Authorities – that require a certain type of information to be protected or restricted in dissemination.

There are two types of CUI Categories and Subcategories: CUI Basic and CUI Specified.

CUI Basic is, as the name implies, the standard "flavor" of CUI.

All of the rules of CUI apply to CUI Basic Categories and Subcategories, making the handling and marking of CUI Basic the simplest.

CUI Specified is different, since the requirements for how users must treat each type of information vary with each Category or Subcategory. This is because some Authorities have VERY specific requirements for how to handle the type of information they pertain to – requirements that simply would not make sense for the rest of CUI.

CUI Specified is NOT a "higher level" of CUI, it is *simply different*. And because the things that make it different are dictated in laws, Federal regulations, and government-wide policies, they are not things that can legally be ignored or overlooked. As such, a document containing multiple CUI Specified Categories and Subcategories must include ALL of them in the CUI Banner Marking.

There is one additional issue with CUI Specified, in that some CUI Categories and Subcategories are only CUI Specified ***sometimes***.

The reason for this is, as stated above, often there are many different laws or regulations that pertain to the same information type, but only *some* of them may include additional or alternate handling requirements from CUI Basic. Therefore, only CUI created under those Authorities would be CUI Specified.

Essentially it comes down to this: If the law, regulation, or Government-wide policy that pertains to your agency is listed in the CUI Registry as a Specified Authority, then you must mark the CUI based in that Authority as CUI Specified and include that marking in the CUI Banner.

Reference: 32 CFR 2002.12 8

Banner Markings (Category or Subcategory Marking)

CUI Category or Subcategory Markings are separated by a double forward slash (//) from the CUI Control Marking. When including multiple CUI Category or Subcategory Markings in the CUI Banner Marking they must be separated by a single forward slash (/).

When a document contains CUI Specified, all CUI Specified Category or Subcategory Markings must be included in the CUI Banner Marking .

Agency heads may approve the use of CUI Basic Category or Subcategory Markings through agency CUI policy. When such agency policy exists, all CUI Basic Category or Subcategory Markings must be included in the CUI Banner Marking.

CUI Specified Category Marking

CONTROLLED//SP-SPECIFIED

Department of Good Works
Washington, D.C. 20006

August 27, 2016

MEMORANDUM FOR THE DIRECTOR

From: Gary Walsh
Chief, Cargo Division

Subject: Examples

We support President Meyer by ensuring that the Government protects and provides proper access to information to advance the national and public interest.

We lead efforts to standardize and assess the management of classified and controlled unclassified information through oversight, policy development, guidance, education, and reporting.

CUI Basic Category Marking (if authorized in agency policy)

CUI//BASIC

Department of Good Works
Washington, D.C. 20006

August 27, 2016

MEMORANDUM FOR THE DIRECTOR

From: Robert Loblaw, Esq
Office of the General Counsel

Subject: Examples

We support Congressman Love by ensuring that the Government protects and provides proper access to information to advance the national and public interest.

We lead efforts to standardize and assess the management of classified and controlled unclassified information through oversight, policy development, guidance, education, and reporting.

NOTE: The above examples use the words "SP-SPECIFIED" and "BASIC" as substitutes for CUI Category and Subcategory Markings. Consult the CUI Registry for actual CUI markings.

Reference: 32 CFR 2002.20(b)(2)

Marking CUI Specified

Since CUI Specified Categories and Subcategories are different – both from CUI Basic and also from each other – CUI Specified MUST always be included in the CUI Banner.

This is done to ensure that every authorized holder and end user who receives a document containing CUI Specified knows that the document must be treated in a manner that differs from CUI Basic.

We accomplish this marking in two ways:

1. All CUI Specified documents must include the Category or Subcategory marking for all of the CUI Specified contained in that document in the CUI Banner Marking. This ensures that the first thing a user in receipt of that document sees is the CUI Banner letting them know they have something other than just CUI Basic and will have to meet any additional or alternative requirements for the CUI Specified they hold.
2. To make sure that it is obvious that a Category or Subcategory is Specified, the marking has "SP-" added to the beginning of it.

"SP-" added to beginning of Category markings from CUI Registry

MANDATORY: CUI Specified Markings must appear in CUI Banner

ED

Department of Good Works
Washington, D.C. 20006

August 27, 2016

MEMORANDUM FOR THE DIRECTOR

From: Elliott Alderson, Chief
Robotics Division

Subject: Examples

We support President Walken by ensuring that the Government protects and provides proper access to information to advance the national and public interest.

We lead efforts to standardize and assess the management of classified and controlled unclassified information through oversight, policy development, guidance, education, and reporting.

CUI//SP-SPECIFIED

Department of Good Works
Washington, D.C. 20006

August 27, 2016

MEMORANDUM FOR THE DIRECTOR

From: Tyrell Wellick
Office of the CTO

Subject: Examples

We support President Walken by ensuring that the Government protects and provides proper access to information to advance the national and public interest.

We lead efforts to standardize and assess the management of classified and controlled unclassified information through oversight, policy development, guidance, education, and reporting.

NOTE: The above examples use the word "SPECIFIED" as a substitute for CUI Category and Subcategory Markings. Consult the CUI Registry for actual CUI markings.

Reference: 32 CFR 2002.20 10

Banner Markings (Multiple Category or Subcategory Marking)

CUI Specified Markings MUST precede CUI Basic Markings (where authorized for use by the agency head) in the CUI Banner. Consult your agency CUI policy for guidance on use of CUI Basic Category or Subcategory Markings.

CUI Category and Subcategory Markings MUST be alphabetized within CUI type (Basic or Specified).

Alphabetized Specified CUI categories and subcategories MUST precede alphabetized Basic CUI categories and subcategories.

Below are examples of CUI Banner Markings used in a document that contains both CUI Specified and CUI Basic

CUI Specified Categories Precede CUI Basic Categories

All Categories are Alphabetized by Type Specified vs. Basic (where use of Basic is authorized)

CUI Specified | **Alphabetized CUI Basic** | **Alphabetized CUI Specified** | **CUI Basic**

CUI// SP-SPECIFIED-C/AAAA/BBBB//DISSEM

Department of Good Works
Washington, D.C. 20006

August 27, 2016

MEMORANDUM FOR THE DIRECTOR

From: Joshua Lyman
Deputy Chief of Staff, Division 5

Subject: Examples

We support President Bartlett by ensuring that the Government protects and provides proper access to information to advance the national and public interest.

CUI// SP-SPECIFIED-A/SP-SPECIFIED-B/AAAA//DISSEM

Department of Good Works
Washington, D.C. 20006

August 27, 2016

MEMORANDUM FOR THE DIRECTOR

From: Dr. Jack Shephard, MD
Chief Health Officer

Subject: Examples

We support President Bartlett by ensuring that the Government protects and provides proper access to information to advance the national and public interest.

NOTE: The above examples use "AAAA" and "BBBB" as substitutes for CUI Basic Category and Subcategory Markings, "SP-SPECIFIED-X" as a substitute for a CUI Specified Category and Subcategory Markings, and "DISSEM" as a substitute for a Limited Dissemination Control Marking. Consult the CUI Registry for actual CUI markings.

Reference: 32 CFR 2002.20

Banner Markings (Limited Dissemination Controls)

Only Limited Dissemination Control Markings found in the CUI Registry are authorized for use with CUI.

Limited Dissemination Control Markings are separated from preceding sections of the CUI Banner Marking by a double forward slash (//).

When a document contains multiple Limited Dissemination Control Markings, those Limited Dissemination Control Markings MUST be alphabetized and separated from each other with a single forward slash (/).

Below are examples that show the proper use of Limited Dissemination Control Markings in the CUI Banner Marking in a letter-type document and a slide presentation.

Limited Dissemination Control Markings

CUI//DISSEM-A/DISSEM-C

Department of Good Works
Washington, D.C. 20006

August 27, 2016

MEMORANDUM FOR THE DIRECTOR

From: William Bailey
Office of the Vice President

Subject: Examples

We support President Santos by ensuring that the Government protects and provides proper access to information to advance the national and public interest.

We lead efforts to standardize and assess the management of classified and controlled unclassified information through oversight, policy development, guidance, education, and reporting.

CONTROLLED//DISSEM-B

Department of Good Works
Washington, D.C. 20006

Marking PowerPoint Slides

HOW TO MARK POWERPOINT SLIDES THAT CONTAIN CUI

CONTROLLED//DISSEM-B

NOTE: The above example uses "DISSEM-X" as a substitute for Limited Dissemination Control Markings. Consult the CUI Registry for actual CUI markings.

Reference: 32 CFR 2002.20(b)(3)

Designation Indicator

All documents containing CUI MUST indicate the designator's agency.

This may be accomplished through the use of letterhead, a signature block with agency, or the use of a "Controlled by" line.

Every effort should be made to identify a point of contact, branch, or division within an organization, and to include contact information.

Below are examples of Designation Indicators in a slide presentation and a letter-type document.

Designating Agency Identification

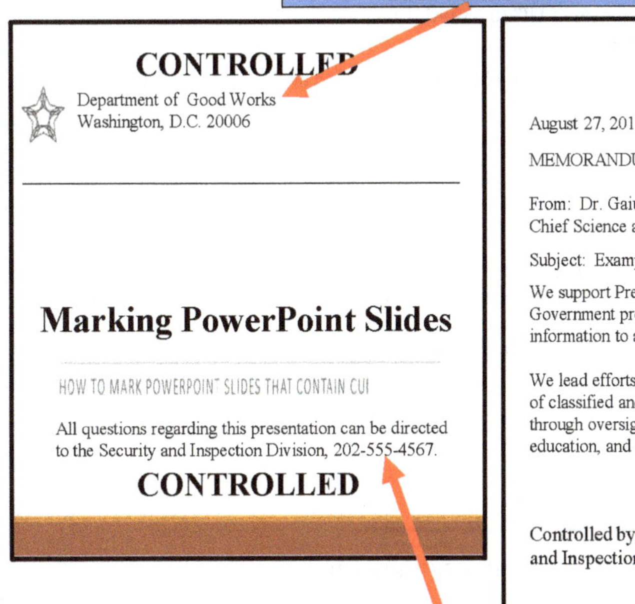

CUI

August 27, 2016

MEMORANDUM FOR THE DIRECTOR

From: Dr. Gaius Baltar
Chief Science and Technology Advisor

Subject: Examples

We support President Roslin by ensuring that the Government protects and provides proper access to information to advance the national and public interest.

We lead efforts to standardize and assess the management of classified and controlled unclassified information through oversight, policy development, guidance, education, and reporting.

"Controlled by:" Line

Controlled by: Department of Good Works, Security and Inspection Division, 202-555-4567.

Contact info

Reference: 32 CFR 2002.20(a)(3)(d)

13

Portion Marking

CUI Portion Marking:

Portion marking of CUI is optional in a fully unclassified document, but is permitted and encouraged to facilitate information sharing and proper handling of the information. Agency heads may approve the required use of CUI Portion marking on all CUI generated within their agency. As such, users should consult their agency CUI policy when creating CUI documents.

When CUI Portion Marking is used, these rules must be followed:

- ❖CUI Portion Markings are placed at the beginning of the portion to which they apply and must be used throughout the entire document.
- ❖CUI Portion Markings are contained within parentheses and may include up to three elements:
    1. The CUI Control Marking: This is mandatory when portion marking and must be the acronym "CUI" (the word "Controlled" will not be used in portion marking).
    2. CUI Category or Subcategory Markings: These can be found in the CUI Registry.
        a. When used, CUI Category or Subcategory Markings are separated from the CUI Control Marking by a double forward slash (//).
        b. When including multiple categories or subcategories in a portion, CUI Category or Subcategory Markings are separated from each other by a single forward slash (/).
    3. Limited Dissemination Control Markings: These can be found in the CUI Registry and are separated from preceding CUI markings by a double forward slash (//). When including multiple Limited Dissemination Control Markings, they must be alphabetized and separated from each other by a single forward slash (/).
- ❖When CUI Portion Markings are used and a portion does not contain CUI, a "U" is placed in parentheses to indicate that the portion contains Uncontrolled Unclassified Information.

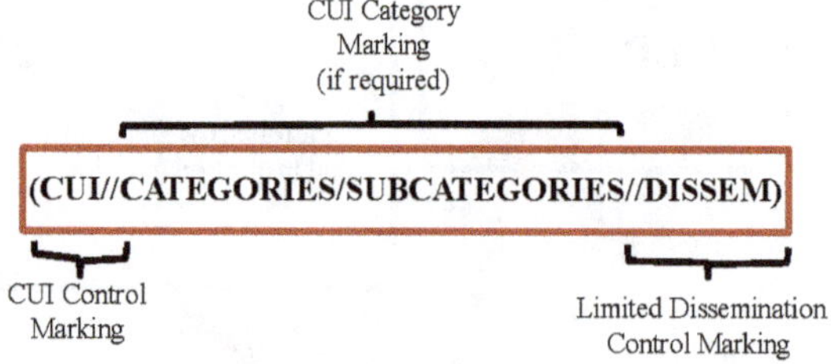

NOTE: The above example uses the words "CATEGORIES" and "SUBCATEGORIES" as substitutes for CUI Category or Subcategory Markings and the word "DISSEM" as a substitute for a Limited Dissemination Control Marking. Consult the CUI Registry for actual CUI markings.

Reference: 32 CFR 2002.20(f) 14

Portion Marking CUI

CUI Portion Markings are placed at the beginning of the portion to which they apply and must be used throughout the entire document. They are presented in all capital letters and separated as indicated in this handbook and the CUI Registry.

The presence of EVEN ONE item of CUI in a document requires CUI marking of that document. Because of this, CUI Portion Markings can be of great assistance in determining if a document contains CUI and therefore must be marked as such.

Remember: When portion markings are used and any portion does not contain CUI, a "(U)" is placed in front of that portion to indicate that it contains Uncontrolled - or non-CUI - Unclassified Information.

CUI Portion Markings

CONTROLLED

Department of Good Works
Washington, D.C. 20006

August 27, 2016

MEMORANDUM FOR THE DIRECTOR

From: Sydney Wade
Chief, Environmental Protection Division

Subject: (CUI) Traffic Patterns of Dupont Circle

(U) We support President Shepard by ensuring that the Government protects and provides proper access to information to advance the national and public interest.

(CUI) For training purposes this paragraph contrails CUI. We lead efforts to standardize and assess the management of classified and controlled unclassified information through oversight, policy development, guidance, education, and reporting.

CONTROLLED

Department of Good Works
Washington, D.C. 20006

August 27, 2016

MEMORANDUM FOR THE DIRECTOR

From: Det. Jonathon McLane
NYPD Liaison Officer

Subject: (U) Examples

(U) We support President Shepard by ensuring that the Government protects and provides proper access to information to advance the national and public interest.

(CUI) For training purposes this paragraph contrails CUI specified. We lead efforts to standardize and assess the management of classified and controlled unclassified information through oversight, policy development, guidance, education, and reporting.

(U) Markings informational only, not carried to CUI Banner

Reference: 32 CFR 2002.20(f) 15

Portion Markings (with Category only)

This example shows how to portion mark a document using the CUI Control Marking and CUI Category or Subcategory Markings.

When a document contains CUI Specified, all CUI Specified Category or Subcategory Markings must be included in the CUI Banner Marking. Consult your agency CUI policy for guidance on use of CUI Basic Category or Subcategory Markings.

Remember: When CUI Portion Markings are used and a portion does not contain CUI, a "U" is placed in parentheses to indicate that the portion contains Uncontrolled Unclassified Information.

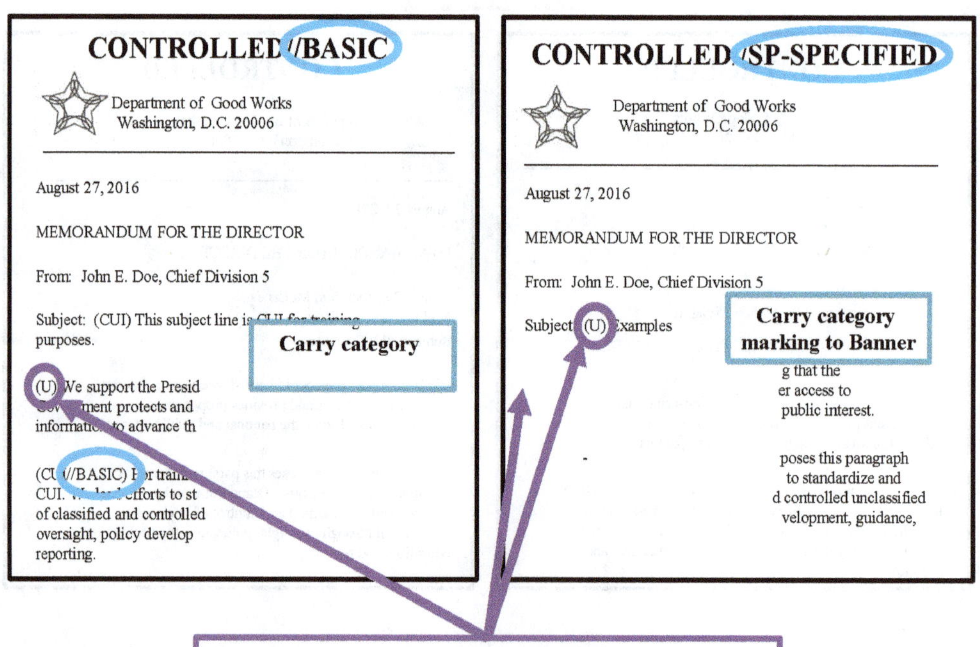

NOTE: The above example uses "BASIC" and "SPECIFIED" as substitutes for CUI Category or Subcategory Markings. Consult the CUI Registry for actual CUI markings.

Reference: 32 CFR 2002.20(f) 16

Portion Markings (with Category and Dissemination)

This example shows how to portion mark a document using all three components of the CUI Banner Marking.

When a document contains CUI Specified, CUI Specified Category or Subcategory Markings must be included in the CUI Banner Marking. Consult your agency CUI policy for guidance on use of CUI Basic Category or Subcategory Markings.

Remember: When CUI Portion Markings are used and a portion does not contain CUI, a "U" is placed in parentheses to indicate that the portion contains Uncontrolled Unclassified Information.

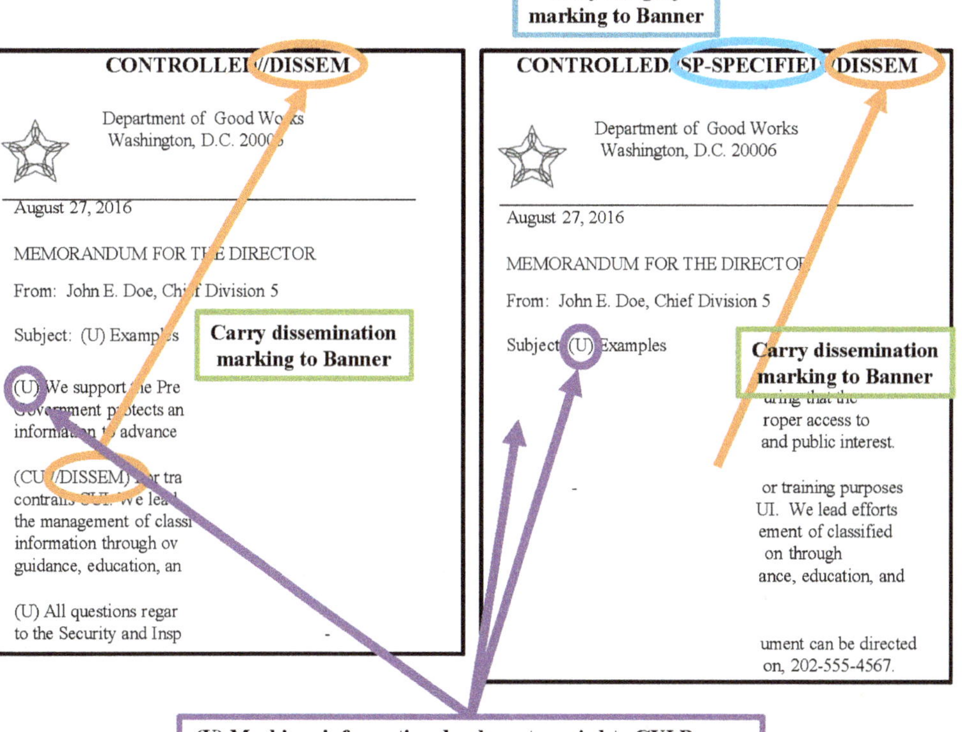

NOTE: The above example uses "SP-SPECIFIED" as a substitute for a CUI Category or Subcategory Marking and "DISSEM" as a substitute for Limited Dissemination Control Markings. Consult the CUI Registry for actual CUI markings.

Reference: 32 CFR 2002.20(f)

COMMON MISTAKES
(Category or Subcategory Markings NOT in Banner Marking)

Remember: Category and Subcategory Markings for CUI Specified MUST always be included in the Banner Marking and those for CUI Basic may be required by agency CUI policy.

Accordingly, when CUI Portion Markings are used and include CUI Category or Subcategory Markings, those markings MUST be included in the CUI Banner Marking.

In this example CUI Specified Category or Subcategory Markings are included in the portion marking but not in the Banner Marking. THIS IS NOT AUTHORIZED.

Department of Goo
Washington, D.C

August 27, 2016

MEMORANDUM FOR THE DIRECTOR

From: John E. Doe, Chief Division 5

Subject: (U) Examples

(U) We support the President by ensuring that the Government protects and provides proper access to information to advance the national and public interest.

(CUI/SP-SPECIFIED DISSEM) For training purposes this paragraph contains specified CUI. We lead efforts to standardize and assess the management of classified and controlled unclassified information through oversight, policy development, guidance, education, and reporting.

(U) All questions regarding this document can be directed to the Security and Inspection Division, 202-555-4567.

NOTE: The above example uses "SP-SPECIFIED" as a substitute for a CUI Specified Category or Subcategory Marking and "DISSEM" as a substitute for a Limited Dissemination Control Marking. Consult the CUI Registry for actual CUI markings.

Marking Multiple Pages

The makeup of the CUI Banner Marking for a multi-page document is essentially the sum of all of the CUI markings in the document. If any portion of the document contains CUI Specified or a Limited Dissemination Control Marking then the CUI Banner Marking must reflect that.
Below is an example of one multi-page document with CUI Portion Marking.

CUI//SP-SPECIFIED-A/SP-SPECIFIED-B//DISSEM

Department of Good Works
Washington, D.C. 20006

August 27, 2016

MEMORANDUM FOR THE DIRECTOR

From: John E Doe, Chief Division

Subject: (U) Examples

(CUI) We support the President by ensuring that the Government protects and provides proper access to information to advance the national and public interest.

1

CUI//SP-SPECIFIED-A/SP-SPECIFIED-B//DISSEM

(CUI//SP-SPECIFIED-A//DISSEM) We lead efforts to standardize and assess the management of classified and controlled unclassified information through oversight, policy development, guidance, education, and reporting.

(U) All questions regarding this document can be directed to the Security and Inspection Division, 202- 555-4567.

(CUI) This bullet contains CUI Basic.

(CUI//SP-SPECIFIED-B) This paragraph contains certain facts.

2

CUI//SP-SPECIFIED-A/SP-SPECIFIED-B//DISSEM

(U) We lead efforts to standardize and assess the management of classified and controlled unclassified information through oversight, policy development, guidance, education, and reporting.

(CUI//SP-SPECIFIED-A) Certain items are here that related to a specified category.

(CUI//DISSEM) Only certain audiences could receive this CUI, as demonstrated by the marking.

3

CUI Banner Marking includes all Specified and Dissem. Markings from throughout document.

CUI//SP-SPECIFIED-A/SP-SPECIFIED-B//DISSEM

(CUI//DISSEM) We lead efforts to standardize and assess the management of classified and controlled unclassified information through oversight, policy development, guidance, education, and reporting.

(CUI//SP-SPECIFIED-B) This bullet includes the conclusion and recommended actions.

4

NOTE: The overall CUI Banner Marking for the document must appear on all pages of the document.

Reference: 32 CFR 2002.20(c)

19

Required Indicators per Authorities

Required indicators – including, informational, warning, or dissemination statements – may be mandated by the law, Federal regulation, or Government-wide policythat makes a specific item of information CUI.

These indicators shall not be included in the CUI Banner or portion markings, but must appear in a manner readily apparent to authorized personnel and consistent with the requirements of the governing document.

Sample Required Indicators

CONTROLLED//SP-SPECIFIED

MARKING REQUIRED PER AUTHORITY

Department of Good Works
Washington, D.C. 20006

August 27, 2016

MEMORANDUM FOR THE DIRECTOR

From: John E. Doe, Chief Division 5

Subject: Examples

We support the President by ensuring that the Government protects and provides proper access to information to advance the national and public interest.

We lead efforts to standardize and assess the management of classified and controlled unclassified information through oversight, policy development, guidance, education, and reporting.

WARNING: These are words required by the authority. This text is stand in text only, please see the CUI Registry and the applicable law regulation or government-wide policy for exact requirements. These are words required by the authority.

NOTE: The above example uses "SPECIFIED" as a substitute for a CUI Specified Category or Subcategory Marking. Consult the CUI Registry for actual CUI markings.

Reference: 32 CFR 2002.20 (b)(2)(iii)

Supplemental Administrative Markings

Agencies may use supplemental administrative markings (e.g., Draft, Deliberative, Pre- decisional, Provisional) along with CUI to inform recipients of the non-final status of documents ONLY when such markings are created and defined in agency policy.

Supplemental administrative markings may not be used to control CUI and may not be commingled with or incorporated into the CUI Banner Marking or Portion Markings. Supplemental administrative markings may not duplicate any marking in the CUI Registry.

Below are two examples of ways to properly use supplemental administrative markings .

CONTROLLED

Department of Good Works
Washington, D.C. 20006

August 27, 2016

MEMORANDUM FOR THE DIRECTOR

From: John E. Doe, Chief Division 5

Subject: Examples

We support the President by ensuring that the Government protects and provides proper access to information to advance the national and public interest.

We lead efforts to standardize and assess the management of classified and controlled unclassified information through oversight, policy development, guidance, education, and reporting.

DRAFT

CUI

PROVISIONAL – IN WORK

Department of Good Works
Washington, D.C. 20006

August 27, 2016

MEMORANDUM FOR THE DIRECTOR
From: John E. Doe, Chief Division 5
Subject: Examples

We support the President by ensuring that the Government protects and provides proper access to information to advance the national and public interest.

We lead efforts to standardize and assess the management of classified and controlled unclassified information through oversight, policy development, guidance, education, and reporting.

Sample Supplemental Administrative Indicators

COMMON MISTAKES (Supplemental Administrative Markings)

Remember: Supplemental administrative markings may not be used to control CUI and must not be incorporated into CUI Banner Markings or CUI Portion Markings, or duplicate any marking in the CUI Registry.

Below are two examples of ways **NOT** to use administrative markings.

In this example DRAFT is used as part of the CUI Banner Marking THIS IS NOT AUTHORIZED.

CONTROLLED//DRAFT

Department of Good Works
Washington, D.C. 20006

August 27, 2016

MEMORANDUM FOR THE DIRECTOR

From: John E. Doe, Chief Division 5

Subject: Examples

We support the President by ensuring that the Government protects and provides proper access to information to advance the national and public interest.

We lead efforts to standardize and assess the management of classified and controlled unclassified information through oversight, policy development, guidance, education, and reporting.

In this example CUI is included as a part of the administrative indicator. THIS IS NOT AUTHORIZED.

Department of Good Works
Washington, D.C. 20006

August 27, 2016

MEMORANDUM FOR THE DIRECTOR

From: John E. Doe, Chief Division 5

Subject: Examples

We support the President by ensuring that the Government protects and provides proper access to information to advance the national and public interest.

We lead efforts to standardize and assess the management of classified and controlled unclassified information through oversight, policy development, guidance, education, and reporting.

CUI DRAFT

Reference: 32 CFR 2002.20(l)

Marking Electronic Media Storing or Processing CUI

Media such as USB sticks, hard drives, and CD ROMs must be marked to alert holders to the presence of CUI stored on the device.

Due to space limitations it may not be possible to include CUI Category, Subcategory, or Limited Dissemination Control Markings. At a minimum, mark media with the CUI Control Marking ("CONTROLLED" or "CUI") and the designating agency.

Removable Hard drive

Equipment can be marked or labeled to indicate that CUI is stored on the device.

NOTE: DOGW is an acronym for Department of Good Works.

Reference: 32 CFR 2002.20 23

Marking Forms with CUI

Forms that contain CUI must be marked accordingly when filled in. If space on the form is limited, cover sheets can be used for this purpose.

As forms are updated during agency implementation of the CUI Program, they should be modified to include a statement that indicates the form is CUI when filled in.

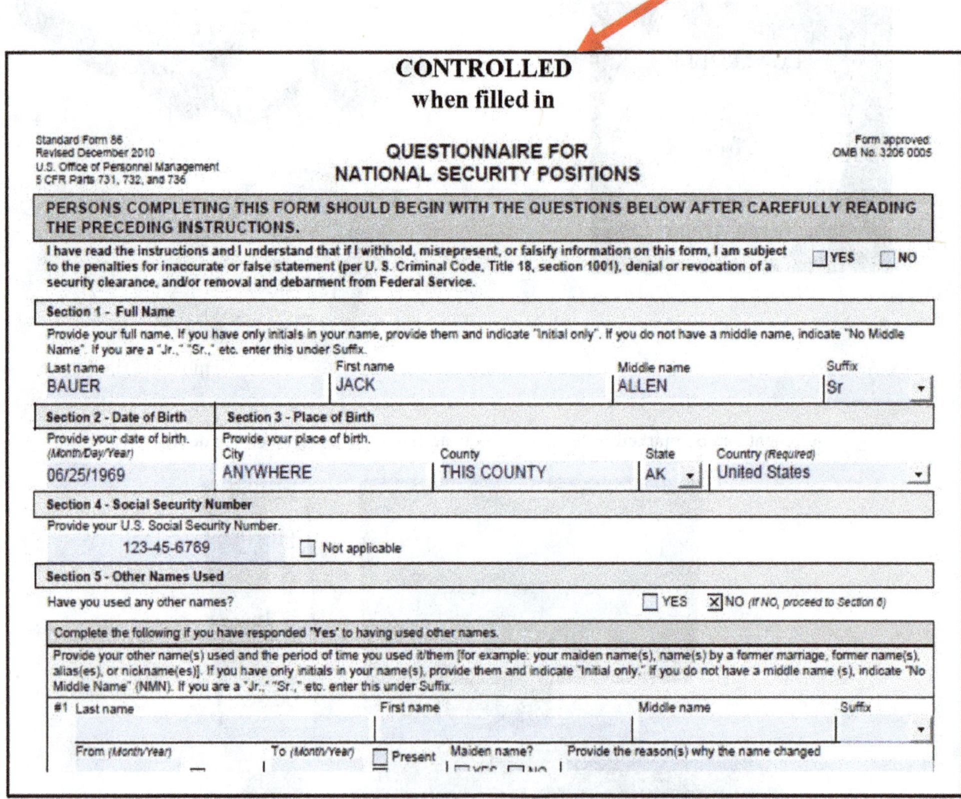

CUI Coversheets

The use of CUI coversheets is optional except when required by agency policy.

Agencies may download coversheets from the CUI Registry or obtain printed copies through General Services Administration (GSA) Global Supply Centers or the GSA Advantage on-line service.

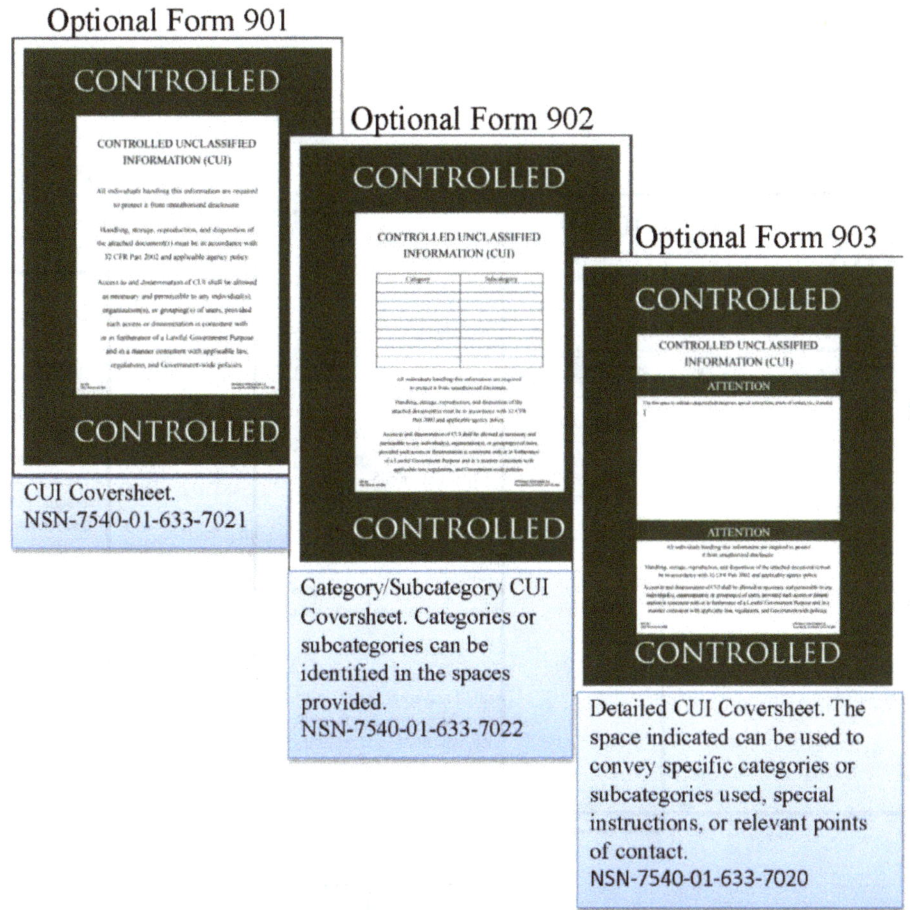

CUI Coversheet. NSN-7540-01-633-7021

Category/Subcategory CUI Coversheet. Categories or subcategories can be identified in the spaces provided. NSN-7540-01-633-7022

Detailed CUI Coversheet. The space indicated can be used to convey specific categories or subcategories used, special instructions, or relevant points of contact. NSN-7540-01-633-7020

Reference: 32 CFR 2002.32

Marking Transmittal Documents

Transmittal document marking requirements:

- When a transmittal document accompanies CUI, the transmittal document must indicate that CUI is attached or enclosed.
- The transmittal document must also include, conspicuously on its face, the following or similar instructions, as appropriate:
  - "When enclosure is removed, this document is Uncontrolled Unclassified Information"; or
  - "When enclosure is removed, this document is (CUI Control Level); upon removal, this document does not contain CUI."

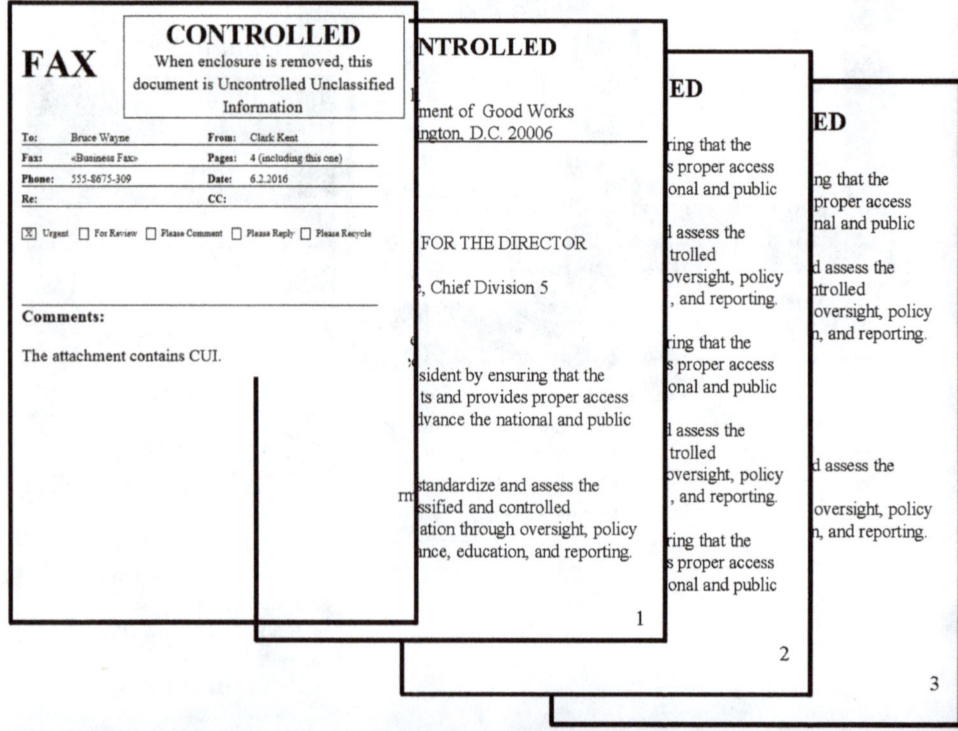

FAX

CONTROLLED
When enclosure is removed, this document is Uncontrolled Unclassified Information

To:	Bruce Wayne	**From:**	Clark Kent
Fax:	«Business Fax»	**Pages:**	4 (including this one)
Phone:	555-8675-309	**Date:**	6.2.2016
Re:		**CC:**	

☒ Urgent ☐ For Review ☐ Please Comment ☐ Please Reply ☐ Please Recycle

Comments:

The attachment contains CUI.

Alternate Marking Methods

Agency heads may authorize the use of alternate marking methods on IT systems, websites, browsers, or databases through agency CUI policy.

These may be used to alert users to the presence of CUI where the agency head has issued a limited CUI marking waiver for CUI designated within the agency.

These warnings may take multiple forms, including the examples on this page. Consult your agency CUI policy for specifics.

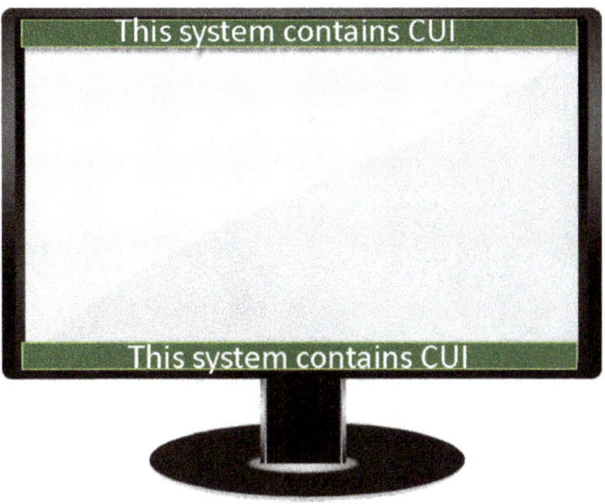

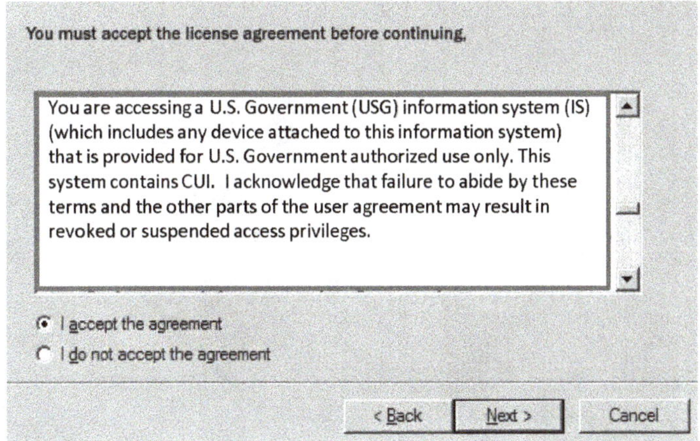

Reference: 32 CFR 2002.20

Room or Area Markings

In areas containing CUI, it may be necessary to alert personnel who are not authorized to access it. This may be accomplished via any means approved by the agency head and detailed in agency CUI policy.

Below is a sample of a sign that indicates CUI is present.

AUTHORIZED
PERSONNEL ONLY

THIS ROOM CONTAINS
CONTROLLED
UNCLASSIFIED
INFORMATION

Reference: 32 CFR 2002.20

Container Markings

When an agency is storing CUI, authorized holders should mark the container to indicate that it contains CUI.

Below are some simple applications of this.

Reference: 32 CFR 2002.20 29

Shipping and Mailing

When shipping CUI:

- Address packages that contain CUI for delivery only to a specific recipient.
- DO NOT put CUI markings on the outside of an envelope or package for mailing/shipping.
- Use in-transit automated tracking and accountability tools where possible.

Agency heads must make sure mail room staff are trained on how to handle CUI, to include reporting any misuse.

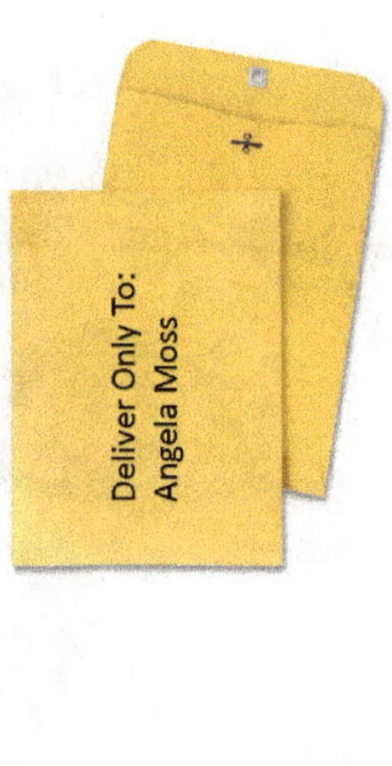

Reference: 32 CFR 2002.20

30

Re-Marking Legacy Information

Legacy information is unclassified information that was marked as restricted from access or dissemination in some way, or otherwise controlled, prior to the CUI Program.

All legacy information is not automatically CUI. Agencies must examine and determine what legacy information qualifies as CUI and mark it accordingly.

In cases of excessive burden, agency heads may issue a "Legacy Marking Waiver," as described in 32 CFR 2002.38(b) of the CUI Rule. When such a waiver is granted by the agency head, legacy material that qualifies need not be remarked as CUI until and unless it is to be "re-used" in a new document.

The process for evaluating legacy material for remarking is contained on the next page.

LEGACY MARKING

Department of Good Works
Washington, D.C. 20006

August 27, 2016

MEMORANDUM FOR THE DIRECTOR

From: John E. Doe, Chief Division 5

Subject: Examples

We support the President by ensuring that the Government protects and provides proper access to information to advance the national and public interest.

We lead efforts to standardize and assess the management of classified and controlled unclassified information through oversight, policy development, guidance, education, and reporting.

NOTE: "LEGACY MARKING" is used as a substitute for any ad hoc, agency markings used to label unclassified information prior to the creation of the CUI Program.

Reference: 32 CFR 2002.36 31

Re-Marking Legacy Information

When legacy information is to be re-used and incorporated into another document of any kind, it must undergo the process described below.

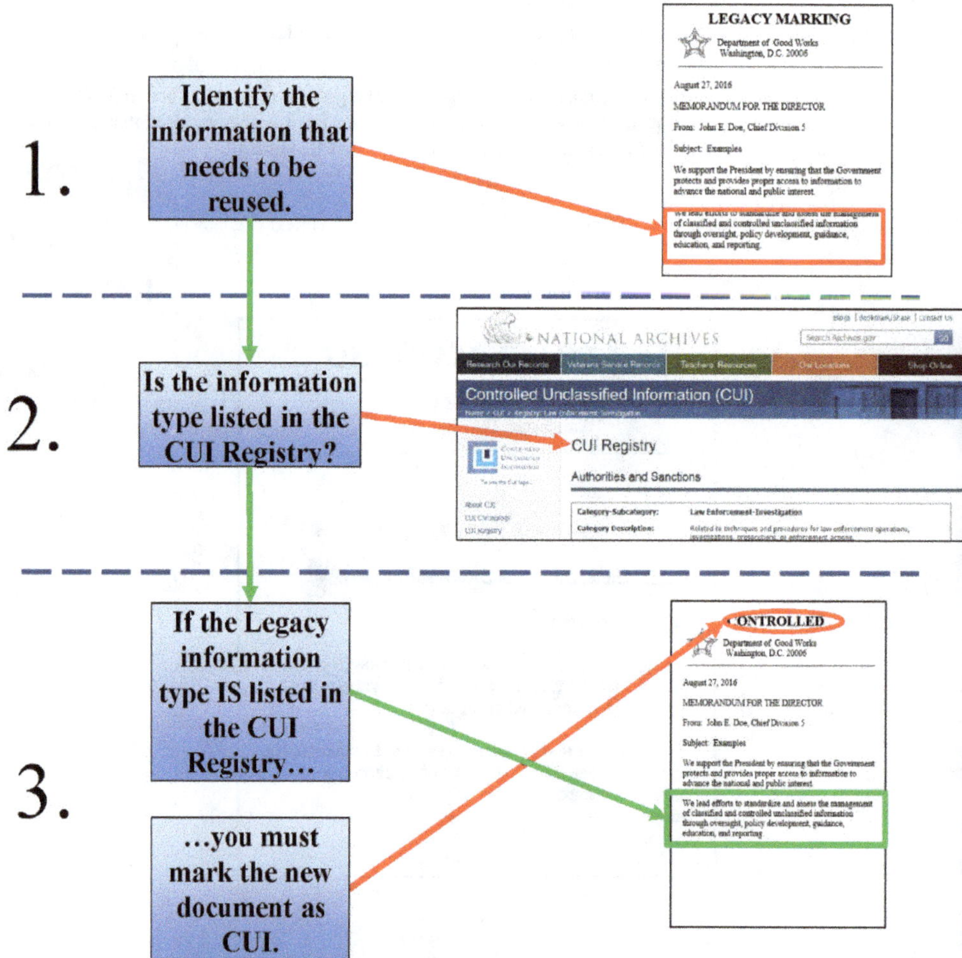

Note: When possible contact the originator of the information for guidance in remarking and protecting the legacy information in the CUI Program.

Reference: 32 CFR 2002.36 32

PART TWO: CUI MARKINGS IN A CLASSIFIED ENVIRONMENT

Marking Commingled Information

- When CUI is included in a document that contains any type of classified information, that document is referred to as "commingled."
- Commingled documents are subject to the requirements of the CUI and Classified National Security Information (CNSI)* Programs.
- As a best practice, keep the CUI and classified information in separate portions to the greatest extent possible to allow for maximum information sharing.
- Mark all portions to ensure that authorized holders can distinguish CUI portions from those containing just CNSI and/or Uncontrolled Unclassified information**.
- The decontrolling provisions for CUI apply only to portions marked as CUI. CNSI portions remain subject to their own declassification requirements.

* Executive Order 13526 – Classified National Security Information.
** Uncontrolled Unclassified information (UUI) is information that neither Executive Order 13556 nor the authorities governing classified information cover as protected. UUI is still subject to agency public release policies.

Reference: 32 CFR 2002.20(g) 34

Commingling – Banner Lines

In the overall marking banner's CUI section, double forward slashes (//) are used to separate major elements and single forward slashes (/) are used to separate sub-elements. The CUI Control Marking ("CUI") appears in the overall banner marking directly before the CUI category and subcategory markings. When there is CUI Specified in the document, CUI Specified category and subcategory marking(s) must appear in the overall banner marking. In accordance with agency policy, if used, the optional CUI Basic category and subcategory markings would appear next. Both CUI Specified and CUI Basic markings are separately alphabetized. The limited dissemination control markings apply to the entire document and the CUI and classified information in it. Placeholders are not used for missing elements or sub-elements.

When used, banner line elements must appear in the following order:

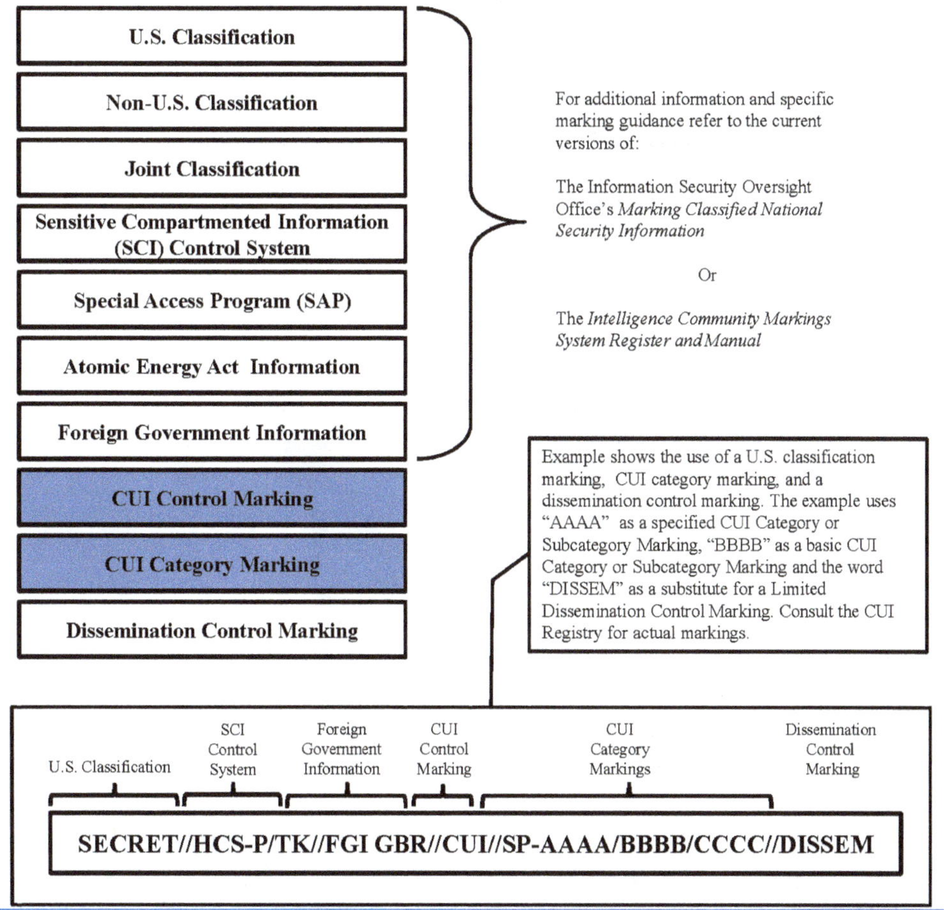

Reference: 32 CFR 2002.20(g)

Commingling – Portion Markings

Although commingling in the same paragraph is not recommended, where paragraphs contain CUI and CNSI commingled, portion marking elements follow a similar syntax to the banner marking:

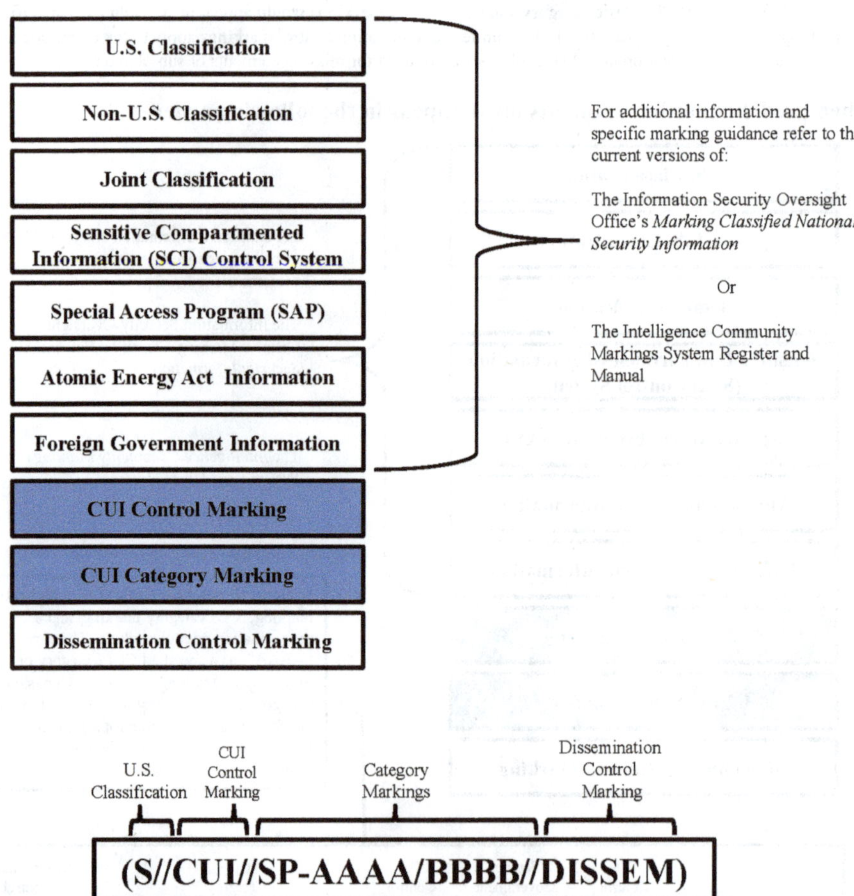

Example shows the use of a U.S. classification, CUI category marking, and a dissemination control marking. The above examples uses "AAAA" as a specified CUI Category or Subcategory Marking, "BBBB" as a basic CUI Category or Subcategory Marking and the word "DISSEM" as a substitute for a Limited Dissemination Control Marking. Consult the CUI Registry for actual markings.

Reference: 32 CFR 2002.20 (g) 36

Commingling Examples (1)

In cases where CUI is commingled with classified information, the following applies:

- In banners, the CUI Control Marking is used only in its abbreviated form ("CUI"). The longer form ("CONTROLLED") is not used.
- Either the classification marking, CUI control marking ("CUI"), or the Uncontrolled Unclassified Marking ("U") must be used in every portion.
  - ✓ **As a best practice, CUI and CNSI should be placed in separate portions.**
- Limited Dissemination Control Markings must appear in the banner line and in all portions to which they apply.

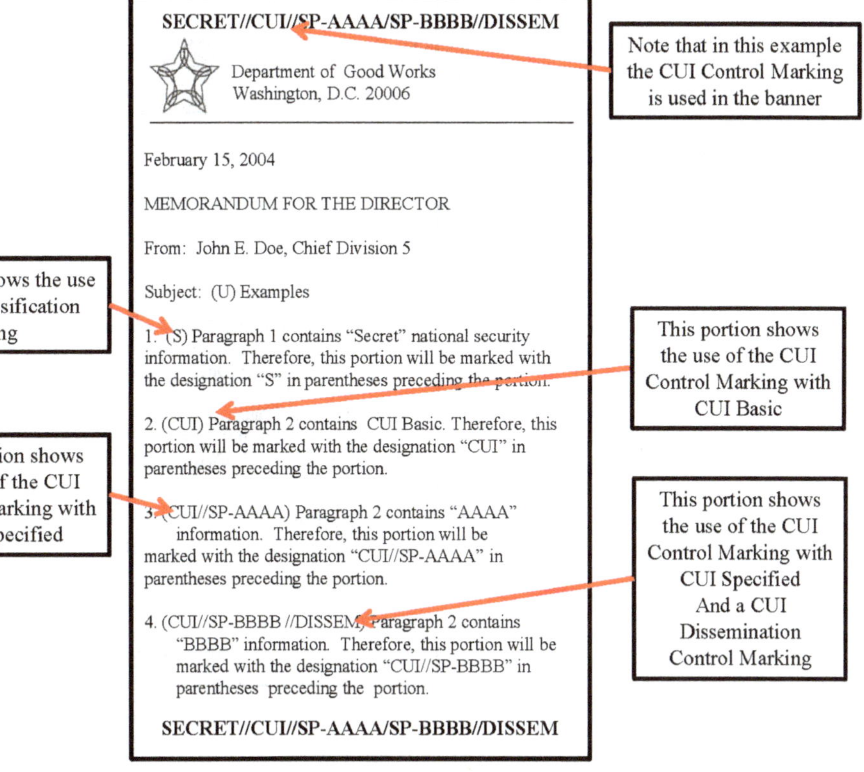

SECRET//CUI//SP-AAAA/SP-BBBB//DISSEM

Department of Good Works
Washington, D.C. 20006

February 15, 2004

MEMORANDUM FOR THE DIRECTOR

From: John E. Doe, Chief Division 5

Subject: (U) Examples

1. (S) Paragraph 1 contains "Secret" national security information. Therefore, this portion will be marked with the designation "S" in parentheses preceding the portion.

2. (CUI) Paragraph 2 contains CUI Basic. Therefore, this portion will be marked with the designation "CUI" in parentheses preceding the portion.

3. (CUI//SP-AAAA) Paragraph 2 contains "AAAA" information. Therefore, this portion will be marked with the designation "CUI//SP-AAAA" in parentheses preceding the portion.

4. (CUI//SP-BBBB //DISSEM) Paragraph 2 contains "BBBB" information. Therefore, this portion will be marked with the designation "CUI//SP-BBBB" in parentheses preceding the portion.

SECRET//CUI//SP-AAAA/SP-BBBB//DISSEM

NOTE: The above examples uses "SP-AAAA" or "SP-BBBB" as CUI Specified Category or Subcategory Markings and the word "DISSEM" as a substitute for a Limited Dissemination Control Marking. Consult the CUI Registry for actual markings.

Reference: 32 CFR 2002.20(g) 37

Commingling Examples (2)

These examples shows the various ways CUI may be identified in a document.

SECRET//CUI

(U) Example of Slide Markings

• (CUI) This bullet contains "Controlled Unc Information." Therefore, this portion will be with the designation "CUI" in parentheses pr the portion.
• (S) This bullet contains "Secret" informat Therefore this portion will be marked with designation "S" in parentheses preceding the

SECRET//CUI

SECRET//CUI//SP-AAAA/SP-BBBB//DISSEM

Department of Good Works
Washington, D.C. 20006

February 15, 2004

MEMORANDUM FOR THE DIRECTOR

From: John E. Doe, Chief Division 5

Subject: (U) Examples

1. (S) Paragraph 1 contains "Secret" national security information. Therefore, this portion will be marked with the designation "S" in parentheses preceding the portion.

2. (CUI//SP-AAAA) Paragraph 2 contains "AAAA" information. Therefore, this portion will be marked with the designation "CUI//SP-AAAA" in parentheses preceding the portion.

3. (CUI//SP-BBBB//DISSEM) Paragraph 2 contains "BBBB" information. Therefore, this portion will be marked with the designation "CUI//SP-BBBB" in parentheses preceding the portion.

SECRET//CUI//SP-AAAA/SP-BBBB//DISSEM

NOTE: The above examples uses "SP-AAAA" or "SP-BBBB" as CUI Specified Category or Subcategory Markings and the word "DISSEM" as a substitute for a Limited Dissemination Control Marking. Consult the CUI Registry for actual markings.

Reference: 32 CFR 2002.20(g) 38

Commingling Examples (3)

Remember: As a best practice, **keep the CUI and classified information in separate portions to the greatest extent possible t**o allow for maximum information sharing.

Below are two samples of CUI commingled with classified information, specifically with Classified National Security Information (CNSI).

The sample on the left has the CUI and CNSI broken into separate paragraphs allowing for easier future separation when needed to accommodate differing access requirements. The sample on the right has CUI and CNSI in the same paragraph.

Recommended Best Practice – Separate CUI and Classified for easier separation when disseminating

SECRET//CUI//SP-AAAA

Department of Good Works
Washington, D.C. 20006

Subject: (CUI) This subject line is CUI for training purposes.

(S) For training purposes this paragraph contains CNSI. We support the President by ensuring that the Government protects and provides proper access to information to advance the national and public interest.

Authorized to combine but requires additional work to separate for dissemination

SECRET//CUI//SP-AAAA

Department of Good Works
Washington, D.C. 20006

Subject: (CUI) This subject line is CUI for training purposes.

(S) For training purposes this paragraph contains CNSI. We support the President by ensuring that the Government protects and provides proper access to information to advance the national and public interest.

(S//CUI//SP-AAAA) For training purposes this paragraph contains CNSI and CUI. We lead efforts to standardize and assess the management of classified and controlled unclassified information through oversight, policy development, guidance, education, and reporting.

(U) All questions regarding this document can be directed to the Security and Inspection Division, 202-555-4567.

Classified By: John E. Doe, Chief Division 5
Reason: 1.4(a)
Declassify on: 20160601

SECRET//CUI//SP-AAAA

NOTE: The above examples use the word "SP-AAAA" as a substitute for a CUI Specified Category or Subcategory Marking. Consult the CUI Registry for actual markings.

Reference: 32 CFR 2002.20(g)

Commingling Portion Marking

In a commingled document, when a portion contains both CUI and classified information, the portion marking for the classified information must precede the CUI Portion Marking.

Remember: When commingling CUI with classified information, the user should keep the CUI and classified portions separate to the greatest extent possible to allow for maximum information sharing. Many of the complex markings seen below can be avoided by following this simple practice.

Below are some examples of how to mark portions containing CUI:

Portion Marking	Contents of Portions Marked Section – CUI ONLY IN PORTION
(CUI)	This section contains CUI Basic.
(CUI//AAAA)	This section contains CUI Basic (with optional category marking).
(CUI//SP-BBBB)	This section contains CUI Specified.
(CUI//SP-BBBB/SP-CCCC)	This section contains two CUI Specified Categories in alphabetical order.
(CUI//DISSEM)	This section contains CUI Basic with a Limited Dissemination Control Marking.
(CUI//AAAA//DISSEM)	This section contains CUI Basic with a Limited Dissemination Control Marking.
(CUI//SP-BBBB//DISSEM)	This section contains CUI Specified with a Limited Dissemination Control Marking.
Portion Marking	**Contents of Portions Marked Section – WITH COMMINGLED PORTIONS (NOT RECOMMENDED)**
(S//CUI)	This section contains Secret information and CUI Basic.
(S//CUI//AAAA)	This section contains Secret information and CUI Basic (with optional category marking).
(S//CUI//SP-BBBB)	This section contains Secret information and CUI Specified.
(S//CUI//SP-BBBB/SP-CCCC)	This section contains Secret information and contains two CUI Specified Categories in alphabetical order.
(S//CUI//SP-BBBB//DISSEM)	This section contains Secret information and CUI Specified with a Limited Dissemination Control Marking.

NOTE: The above examples use “AAAA” as a substitute for a basic CUI Category or Subcategory Marking and “BBBB” or “CCCC” as specified CUI Category or Subcategory Markings and the word “DISSEM” as a substitute for a Limited Dissemination Control Marking. Consult the CUI Registry for actual markings.

Reference: 32 CFR 2002.20(g)

Commingling Portion Marking

In a commingled document, when a portion contains both CUI and classified information, the portion marking for the classified information must precede the CUI Portion Marking.

Remember: When commingling CUI with classified information, the user should keep the CUI and classified portions separate to the greatest extent possible to allow for maximum information sharing. Many of the complex markings seen below can be avoided by following this simple practice.

Below are some examples of how to mark portions containing CUI:

Portion Marking	Contents of Portions Marked Section – CUI ONLY IN PORTION
(CUI)	This section contains CUI Basic.
(CUI//AAAA)	This section contains CUI Basic (with optional category marking).
(CUI//SP-BBBB)	This section contains CUI Specified.
(CUI//SP-BBBB/SP-CCCC)	This section contains two CUI Specified Categories in alphabetical order.
(CUI//DISSEM)	This section contains CUI Basic with a Limited Dissemination Control Marking.
(CUI//AAAA//DISSEM)	This section contains CUI Basic with a Limited Dissemination Control Marking.
(CUI//SP-BBBB//DISSEM)	This section contains CUI Specified with a Limited Dissemination Control Marking.
Portion Marking	**Contents of Portions Marked Section – WITH COMMINGLED PORTIONS (NOT RECOMMENDED)**
(S//CUI)	This section contains Secret information and CUI Basic.
(S//CUI//AAAA)	This section contains Secret information and CUI Basic (with optional category marking).
(S//CUI//SP-BBBB)	This section contains Secret information and CUI Specified.
(S//CUI//SP-BBBB/SP-CCCC)	This section contains Secret information and contains two CUI Specified Categories in alphabetical order.
(S//CUI//SP-BBBB//DISSEM)	This section contains Secret information and CUI Specified with a Limited Dissemination Control Marking.

NOTE: The above examples use "AAAA" as a substitute for a basic CUI Category or Subcategory Marking and "BBBB" or "CCCC" as specified CUI Category or Subcategory Markings and the word "DISSEM" as a substitute for a Limited Dissemination Control Marking. Consult the CUI Registry for actual markings.

Reference: 32 CFR 2002.20(g)

Information Security Oversight Office
National Archives Building
700 Pennsylvania Avenue, NW
Washington, DC 20408

Phone: 202-357-5250
Fax: 202-357-5907
E-mail: cui@nara.gov
Web page: *www.archives.gov/cui*

NARA CUI FAQs

CUI Frequently Asked Questions[1]

The Controlled Unclassified Information (CUI) blog is an educational and informative resource, run by the CUI Executive Agent, to support the implementation of the CUI Program. Please visit the CUI blog for frequently asked questions and to learn more about the program.

Q&As for the CUI Program *In all cases, refer to your agency's CUI program office for agency-specific requirements.*

---

1. Question: Will unclassified contracts have DD 254s issued to provide CUI Guidance or will unclassified contracts have simple attachments similar to the current FOUO (For Official Use Only) for guidance?

> **Answer:** DD 254s are only to be used with contracts that include CNSI (Classified National Security Information) requirements. The CUI EA has been working to develop a FAR (Federal Acquisitions Regulation) case (with GSA, DoD, NASA, DHS) that will be used to standardize the way Executive branch agencies convey safeguarding guidance for CUI. This FAR case includes a draft standard form, similar to the DD 254, that is intended to consolidate where contract-related CUI requirements are conveyed).

[1] Copied from https://www.archives.gov/cui/faqs.html. Numbers have been added to each question for easier reference in the text of the CUI Informed book. No other changes have been made.

2. Question: Who is the responsible party for issuing Legacy CUI marking waivers?

> **Answer:** Per 32 CFR 2002.38, Senior Agency Officials (SAO) may issue marking waivers for CUI while it remains under agency control.

3. Question: Where is the agency CUI POC list?

> **Answer:** https://www.archives.gov/cui/about/contact.html#contact-an-agency

4. Question: Who is responsible for marking CUI? The CUI EA (ISOO) has run into agencies failing to do so. If we don't generate the material what is contractor responsibility?

> **Answer:** Upon implementation, agencies are responsible for marking or identifying any CUI shared with non-federal entities. Questions regarding the status of information (marked or unmarked) should be directed back to the government contracting activity. Some agencies are not yet marking CUI and are still implementing the elements of the CUI program. Contractors should not follow CUI program requirements or markings until directed to do so in a contract or agreement.

5. Question: Would you please define agency when discussing legacy information?

Answer: An agency (also a Federal agency, an executive agency, executive branch agency) is any "executive agency," as defined in 5 U.S.C. 105; the United States Postal Service; and any other independent entity within the executive branch that designates or handles CUI.

6. Question: What do you consider a re-use of CUI?

Answer: Re-use means incorporating, restating, or paraphrasing information from its originally designated form into a newly created document.

7. Question: What's the difference between CUI and Controlled?

Answer: There is no difference. Both are authorized CUI Control Markings and can be used interchangeably unless limited by agency policy

8. Question: Why is there, not a marking equivalent to "RELIDO" (which is an intelligence marking that allows authorized people downstream to further disseminate as needed without going back to the originator)?

Answer: The only authorized Limited Dissemination Control (LDC) markings that can be used with CUI are those found on the CUI Registry. CUI Notice 2018-07 (https://www.archives.gov/files/cui/documents/20181116-cui-notice-2018-07-limited-dissemination-controls.pdf) describes the proper use of LDC, along with the process for submitting new/additional LDCs for use with CUI. The dissemination of all

CUI is governed by the principle of "Lawful Government Purpose". This means that any recipient of CUI is deemed to have a mission-related purpose to receive the information and that there must be no prohibition to that dissemination in law, regulation, or governmentwide policy. If an agency wishes to communicate a restriction beyond this, any of the above-mentioned dissemination controls can be applied as appropriate.

9. Question: Can you give examples of CUI Basic?

Answer: The CUI Registry lists all authorized CUI Categories (basic and specified), which is located at https://www.archives.gov/cui/registry/category-marking-list. The categories on this page that do not have a marking with "SP-" are CUI basic categories, like the agriculture category and the asylee category.

10. Question: Does Industry ever have to mark CUI?

Answer: Yes, but only when instructed to do so in the contract or supporting documentation, and have a lawful government purpose to do so.

11. Question: Should a company be concerned with protecting CUI that is received from a government customer?

Answer: CUI must be safeguarded in accordance with the contract, whether it is created or collected for the government, or shared from the government to the contractor.

12. Question: When it comes to legacy information, should a contractor/company wait until the government agency (they work for/with) sends new documents that are marked CUI?

Answer: Any information received or created as part of a current or previous contract should be protected in accordance with the terms of the contract under which it was received or created. As agencies implement, CUI requirements will be added to existing and new contracts.

13. Question: What should be done if a customer marks every document CONTROLLED with no true banner marking? Is that considered Basic? The word Controlled is an authorized banner marking for Basic CUI.

Answer: Under the CUI program, information marked "CONTROLLED" (CONTROLLED is a true banner marking) without additional markings would be CUI basic. Confirm with your customer and your contract that they are using CUI markings and ensure you follow any and all requirements in your contract or agreement.

14. Question: How do you navigate a situation where you feel you have CUI but it hasn't been marked appropriately?

Answer: Questions regarding the status of CUI should be directed to the originator of the information or the government contracting activity.

15. Question: What is the difference between U//FOUO and CUI?

Answer: U//FOUO is a legacy marking used to indicate sensitivity based on agency policy or practice. CUI is a marking that is used to indicate the presence of CUI basic information. CUI markings are applied only to those information types/categories found on the CUI Registry and can be linked to laws, regulations, or Government-wide policies calling for protection or control of the information. As the CUI program is implemented, U//FOUO will cease to be an authorized marking, but may still be seen on legacy documents once the transition to CUI is complete.

16. Question: Banner Marking and document marking work for unstructured data? What about marking structured data such as databases?

Answer: For databases or applications, splash screens or banner marking can be used to satisfy the marking and identification requirements of the CUI Program. System outputs can also be modified to apply markings upon printing or downloading from the application.

The CUI office is working with NIEM to create a CUI Metadata standard that can be used to indicate CUI markings. Updates on this project will be relayed on the CUI Blog.

17. Question: Do you mark/tag fields in the Database or categorize the system itself?

Answer: Individual fields can be marked or a general alert can be placed on entry into the database/system (such as a splash screen and/or a banner at the top of the screen). System outputs should be modified to include applicable CUI markings as needed, you can also use the CUI cover sheet SF901 when printing.

18. Question: How would I mark/tag a system?

Answer: Please refer to the CUI Marking handbook, page 27

19. Question: Is purple recommended, but not required for the CUI cover sheet?

Answer: The SF 901 is purple. If color printing is not available, the form can be printed in black and white. The CUI cover (OF 901, 902, 903) sheet used to be green and should not be used; it has been replaced with the SF 901.

20. Question: Do contractors have to mark CUI if their contract requires it?

Answer: Yes. Contractors need to follow what is in their contracts. CUI requirements do not bind the public, except as authorized by a law, regulation, or as incorporated into a contract or agreement.

21. Question: Are there reporting requirements and corrective actions for a CUI spillage, similar to those present for classified information?

Answer: Agencies should develop reporting requirements for CUI spillage incidents. Certain categories of CUI, like privacy, have special reporting requirements for loss or incidents.

22. Question: Is the CUI banner marking replacing anything that we would have labeled FOUO?

Answer: Once agencies implement the CUI program, legacy markings such as FOUO or SBU will no longer be used. In some cases, what was previously marked as FOUO would align and be marked as CUI.

23. Question: How should Industry label their computers or USBs containing CUI?

Answer: SF 902s and SF 903s can be used by Industry to label hard drives or USBs (media) that contain CUI. They can be ordered from GSA here https://www.gsaadvantage.gov/. You can also use a splash screen when signing in or a banner at the top/bottom of the screen to alert the user that there is CUI on the network being used.

24. Question: If there are questions in regards to ITAR controls, does the CUI website offer any help and where can we find it?

Answer: Please see the Export Control Category of CUI. https://www.archives.gov/cui/registry/category-detail/export-control.html

25. Question: Do Industry personnel have the authority to generate original CUI?

Answer: Depending on the terms of the contract, Industry may have the authority to generate CUI on behalf of the USG.

26. Question: What's the difference between CUI, FOUO, and the Privacy Act Coversheets?

Answer: The SF 901, CUI coversheet is authorized for use with CUI. Upon the implementation of the CUI Program for an agency, coversheets that are not required per underlying authorities, such as FOUO and Privacy Act, may no longer be used.

27. Question: Where can subcontractors get CUI requirements?

Answer: The Draft CUI FAR case will have flowdown requirements much like the DFARs 252.204-7012. Flowdown requirements should be reflected in the contract.

28. Question: Are you familiar with any solutions that can automate the process of e-mail marking?

Answer: ISOO is aware of a number of efforts within the Industry and within agencies to develop automated/assisted marking solutions for CUI. There are no plans at this time by ISOO to publish an evaluated or approved list of vendors who have developed automated/assisted marking tools for CUI.

29. Question: Can the CUI coversheet be used instead of marking each page of the document, or do we need to

Answer: An SF 901 may be used in lieu of marking every page of a document. Be sure to list on the SF 901 any specified categories, limited dissemination controls, or requirements called for by laws, regulations, or government-wide policies.

30. Question: Is it required that CUI be stored in a GSA-approved safe?

Answer: No. CUI must be stored behind a locking barrier inside a controlled environment that prevents unauthorized access. Organizations have some flexibility in determining what qualifies as a controlled environment. CUI-specified categories may have additional physical security requirements.

31. Question: Where can we access the CUI Marking Handbook?

Answer: https://www.archives.gov/files/cui/documents/20161206-cui-marking-handbook-v1-1-20190524.pdf

32. Question: What is the mechanism for removing markings or lifting restrictions on documents if/when the restriction has expired or no longer applies?

Answer: CUI markings can be removed when the information has been decontrolled. Decontrolling occurs when an authorized holder, consistent with 32 CFR 2002 and the CUI Registry, removes safeguarding or dissemination controls from CUI that no longer require such controls. Decontrol may occur automatically or through agency action. See 32 CFR § 2002.18.

33. Question: Are there specific/special record retention issues/timeframes specific to CUI?

Answer: No. Records retention issues/timeframes are not impacted by a record's status as CUI.

34. Question: As a contractor with DoD, where can I go with CUI questions?

Answer: For compliance with DoD contracts, the first place to check is the contract itself or the POC for the contract. For questions about compliance with DFARs 7012, check out the DoD Procurement Toolbox at: https://dodprocurementtoolbox.com/faqs/cybersecurity/cybersecurity-faqs . E-mail osd.dibcsia@mail.mil for clarification on DFARS 252.204-7012 or NIST SP 800-171 in support of DFARS 252.204-7012. Emails sent to that address are reviewed frequently and distributed as appropriate to a cross-functional team of subject matter experts for action.

DoDI 5200.48 – Controlled Unclassified Information (CUI)

DoDI 5200.48

DoD Instruction 5200.48

Controlled Unclassified Information (CUI)

Originating Component:	Office of the Under Secretary of Defense for Intelligence and Security
Effective:	March 6, 2020
Releasability:	Cleared for public release. Available on the Directives Division Website at https://www.esd.whs.mil/DD/.
Cancels:	DoD Manual 5200.01, Volume 4, "DoD Information Security Program: Controlled Unclassified Information," February 24, 2012, as amended
Approved by:	Joseph D. Kernan, Under Secretary of Defense for Intelligence and Security (USD(I&S))

Purpose: In accordance with the authority in DoD Directive (DoDD) 5143.01 and the December 22, 2010 Deputy Secretary of Defense Memorandum, this issuance:

- Establishes policy, assigns responsibilities, and prescribes procedures for CUI throughout the DoD in accordance with Executive Order (E.O.) 13556; Part 2002 of Title 32, Code of Federal Regulations (CFR); and Defense Federal Acquisition Regulation Supplement (DFARS) Sections 252.204-7008 and 252.204-7012.
- Establishes the official DoD CUI Registry.

TABLE OF CONTENTS

TABLES

FIGURES

SECTION 1: GENERAL ISSUANCE INFORMATION

1.1. APPLICABILITY.

This issuance applies to:

a. Office of the Secretary of Defense (OSD), the Military Departments, the Office of the Chairman of the Joint Chiefs of Staff and the Joint Staff, the Combatant Commands, the Office of the Inspector General of the Department of Defense (OIG DoD), the Defense Agencies, the DoD Field Activities, and all other organizational entities within the DoD (referred to collectively in this issuance as the "DoD Components").

b. Arrangements, agreements, contracts, and other transaction authority actions requiring access to CUI according to terms and conditions of such documents, as defined in Clause 2.101 of the Federal Acquisition Regulation and Section 2002.4 of Title 32, CFR, including, but not limited to, grants, licenses, certificates, memoranda of agreement/arrangement or understanding, and information-sharing agreements or arrangements.

1.2. POLICY.

It is DoD policy that:

a. As part of the phased DoD CUI Program implementation process endorsed by the CUI Executive Agent (EA) pursuant to Information Security Oversight Office (ISOO) Memorandum dated August 21, 2019, the designation, handling, and decontrolling of CUI (including CUI identification, sharing, marking, safeguarding, storage, dissemination, destruction, and records management) will be conducted in accordance with this issuance and Sections 252.204-7008 and 252.204-7012 of the DFARS when applied by a contract to non-DoD systems.

b. All DoD CUI must be controlled until authorized for public release in accordance with DoD Instructions (DoDIs) 5230.09, 5230.29, and 5400.04, or DoD Manual (DoDM) 5400.07. Official DoD information that is not classified or controlled as CUI will also be reviewed prior to public release in accordance with DoDIs 5230.09 or5230.29.

c. Information will not be designated CUI in order to:

(1) Conceal violations of law, inefficiency, or administrative error.

(2) Prevent embarrassment to a person, organization, or agency.

(3) Prevent open competition.

(4) Control information not requiring protection under a law, regulation, or government-wide policy, unless approved by the CUI EA at the National Archives and Records Administration (NARA), through the Under Secretary of Defense for Intelligence and Security (USD(I&S)).

d. In accordance with the DoD phased CUI Program implementation, all documents containing CUI must carry CUI markings in accordance with this issuance.

e. Although DoD Components are not required to use the terms "Basic" or "Specified" to characterize CUI at this time, DoD Components will apply:

(1) At least the minimum safeguards required to protect CUI.

(2) Terms and specific marking requirements will be promulgated by the USD(I&S) in future guidance.

f. Nothing in this issuance alters or supersedes the existing authorities of the Director of National Intelligence (DNI) regarding CUI.

g. Nothing in this issuance will infringe on the OIG DoD's statutory independence and authority, as articulated in the Inspector General Act of 1978 in the Title 5, United States Code (U.S.C.) Appendix. In the event of any conflict between this instruction and the OIG DoD's statutory independence and authority, the Inspector General Act of 1978 in the Title 5, U.S.C. Appendix takes precedence.

SECTION 2: RESPONSIBILITIES

2.1. USD(I&S)

The USD(I&S):

a. As the DoD Senior Agency Official for Security, establishes policy and oversees the DoD Information Security Program.

b. In coordination with the requesting DoD Component, submits changes to CUI categories on behalf of DoD Components to the CUI EA at NARA.

c. Provides reports to the CUI EA on the DoD CUI Program status, as described in Paragraph 3.6.c., in accordance with Part 2002 of Title 32, CFR.

d. Establishes protocol for resolving disputes about implementing or interpreting E.O. 13556, Part 2002 of Title 32, CFR, the CUI Registry, and this issuance, within and between the DoD Components.

e. Coordinates with the Department of Defense Chief Information Officer (DoD CIO) on CUI waiver requests for DoD information systems (IS) and networks.

f. Coordinates with the CUI EA on DoD Component CUI waiver requests.

2.2. DIRECTOR FOR DEFENSE INTELLIGENCE (COUNTERINTELLIGENCE, LAW ENFORCEMENT, AND SECURITY (DDI(CL&S)).

The DDI(CL&S):

a. Oversees and manages the DoD CUI Program.

b. Reviews and signs all reports and other correspondence related to the DoD CUI Program.

c. Coordinates with the Secretaries of the Military Departments, Under Secretary of Defense for Research and Engineering (USD(R&E)), Under Secretary of Defense for Acquisition and Sustainment (USD(A&S)), and the DoD Component heads to:

(1) Recommend changes to national CUI policy relating to identifying, safeguarding, disseminating, marking, storing, transmitting, reviewing, transporting, re-using, decontrolling, and destroying CUI, and responding to unauthorized disclosure (UD) of CUI.

(2) Review and provide guidance on DoD Component implementation policy and CUI-related matters.

d. Assists the USD(I&S) with overseeing the CUI policy and program execution via the Defense Security Enterprise Executive Committee in accordance with DoDD 5200.43.

e. In coordination with the DoD CIO, USD(A&S), and USD(R&E), provides guidance on implementing uniform standards to display TOP SECRET, SECRET, CONFIDENTIAL, and UNCLASSIFIED for CNSI and CUI controls and banners for DoD systems and networks.

2.3. DIRECTOR, DEFENSE COUNTERINTELLIGENCE AND SECURITY AGENCY (DSCA).

Under the authority, direction, and control of the USD(I&S) and in addition to the responsibilities in Paragraph 2.10., the Director, DCSA:

a. Administers the DoD CUI Program for contractually established CUI requirements for contractors in classified contracts in accordance with the May 17, 2018 Under Secretary of Defense for Intelligence Memorandum.

b. Assesses contractor compliance with contractually established CUI system requirements in DoD classified contracts associated with the National Industrial Security Program (NISP) in accordance with Part 2003 of Title 32, CFR and National Institute of Standards and Technology Special Publication (NIST SP) 800-171 guidelines.

c. Establishes and maintains a process to notify the DoD CIO, USD(R&E), and USD(A&S) of threats related to CUI for further dissemination to DoD Components and contractors in accordance with the Section 252.204-7012 of the DFARS.

d. Provides, in coordination with the USD(I&S), security education, training, and awareness on the required topics identified in Section 2002.30 of Title 32, CFR, including protection and management of CUI, to DoD personnel and contractors through the Center for Development of Security Excellence (CDSE).

e. Provides security assistance and guidance to the DoD Components on the protection of CUI when DoD Components establish CUI requirements in DoD classified contracts for NISP contractors falling under DCSA security oversight.

f. Serves as the DoD-lead to report UDs of CUI, except for the reporting of cyber incidents in accordance with Section 252.204-7012 of the DFARS, associated with contractually established CUI system requirements in DoD classified contracts for NISP contractors falling under DCSA security oversight.

g. Coordinates with the DoD CIO to implement uniform security requirements when the IS or network security controls for unclassified and classified information are included in DoD classified contracts for NISP contractors falling under DCSA security oversight.

h. Consolidates DoD Component input on the oversight of CUI protection requirements in DoD classified contracts for NISP contractors under DCSA security oversight, as required by Information Security Oversight Office (ISOO) Notice 2016-01.

2.4. CHIEF MANAGEMENT OFFICER OF THE DEPARTMENT OF DEFENSE (CMO).

In addition to the responsibilities in Paragraph 2.10., the CMO:

a. Serves as the subject matter expert on CUI containing personally identifiable information and its release in accordance with Subsection 552 of Chapter 5 of Title 5, United States Code (U.S.C.), also known as and referred to in this issuance as the "Freedom of Information Act (FOIA)," implemented through DoDD 5400.07 and DoDI 5400.11, and Subsection 552a of Chapter 5 of Title 5, U.S.C., also known and referred to in the issuance as the "Privacy Act of 1974."

b. Supports OSD with information security matters, as appropriate.

2.5. PFPA.

Under the authority, direction, and control of the CMO, through the Director for Administration and Organizational Policy, and in addition to the responsibilities in Paragraph 2.10., the Director PFPA:

a. Provides information security administrative support to OSD.

b. Provides information on OSD CUI Program status and other formally requested assistance to the USD(I&S) to support the CUI Program.

c. Conducts CUI staff assistance visits to OSD in the National Capital Region.

2.6. UNDER SECRETARY OF DEFENSE FOR POLICY.

In addition to the responsibilities in Paragraph 2.10., the Under Secretary of Defense for Policy:

a. Establishes policy and procedures for disclosing DoD CUI to foreign governments, the North Atlantic Treaty Organization, and international organizations based on formally signed agreements and arrangements between the parties.

b. Requires CUI to be identified in international agreements, arrangements, and contracts having licensing export controls for foreign partners.

2.7. USD(A&S).

In addition to the responsibilities in Paragraph 2.10., pursuant to Section 133b of Title 10, U.S.C., and in coordination with the USD(I&S), DoD CIO, and USD(R&E), the USD(A&S):

a. Maintains, in accordance with Section 252.204-7012 of the DFARS, DoD acquisition contracting processes, policies, and procedures for safeguarding DoD CUI in DoD procurement arrangements, agreements, and contracts, including other transaction authority actions.

b. Supports the development and implementation of a Federal Acquisition Regulation clause applying CUI requirements to defense contractors.

2.8. USD(R&E).

In addition to the responsibilities in Paragraph 2.10., pursuant to Section 133a of Title 10, U.S.C., and in coordination with USD(I&S), the USD(R&E):

a. Establishes DoD CUI processes, policies, and procedures for grants and cooperative research and development arrangements, agreements, and contracts involving controlled technical information (CTI).

b. Establishes a standard process to identify CTI; guidelines for sharing, marking, safeguarding, storing, disseminating, decontrolling, and destroying CTI; and CTI records management requirements contained in contracts, as appropriate.

c. Oversees and ensures DoD CUI guidelines and requirements for sharing, marking, safeguarding, storage, dissemination, decontrol, destruction, and records management of all research, development, test, and evaluation information are properly executed for all DoD owned records.

d. In coordination with the USD(A&S), ensures:

(1) Contracts, arrangements, and agreements for research, development, testing, and evaluation identify CUI at the time of award.

(2) USD(R&E) international agreements, arrangements, and contracts with foreign partners identify CUI within the documents.

(3) DoD Components concluding international agreements, arrangements, and contracts with foreign partners include U.S. Government-approved text on CUI.

2.9. DOD CIO.

In addition to the responsibilities in Paragraph 2.10., the DoD CIO:

a. Oversees CUI metadata tagging standards, consistent with federal data tagging approaches in accordance with the National Strategy for Information Sharing and Safeguarding, to implement the marking requirements in Paragraph 3.4.c. and in accordance with DoDI 8320.07.

b. Integrates CUI metadata tagging standards into DoD information technology content management tools to support discovery, access, auditing, safeguarding, and records management decisions regarding CUI (including monitoring CUI data for visibility, accessibility, trust, interoperability, and comprehension).

c. Provides policy and standards recommendations to the USD(I&S) on updates for the sharing, marking, safeguarding, storage, dissemination, decontrol, destruction, and records management of DoD CUI residing on both DoD and non-DoD IS in accordance with DoDI 8582.01.

d. Oversees Defense Industrial Base Cybersecurity Activities, using the DoD Cyber Crime Center as the single DoD focal point for receiving and disseminating all cyber incident reports impacting unclassified networks of defense contractors.

e. Coordinates with the USD(I&S), USD(A&S), USD(R&E), and DoD Component heads to develop uniform security requirements for industry partners' IS and network security controls adequate for the type of CUI identified in the contract in accordance with Part 2002 of Title 32, CFR, Section 252.204-7012 of the DFARS, and NIST SP 800-171.

f. Coordinates with the Director, DCSA to implement uniform security requirements when IS or network security controls for unclassified and classified information are included in DoD classified contracts of NISP contractors falling under DCSA security oversight.

g. Coordinates with the USD(I&S) to:

(1) Implement information security policy standards for markings to display, CUI for DoD classified and unclassified systems and networks.

(2) Integrate training on safeguarding and handling CUI into updates to initial and annual cybersecurity awareness training.

h. Notifies the CUI EA in coordination with the USD(I&S) of CUI waivers impacting IS or networks in accordance with Title 32 of the CFR.

i. Oversees and ensures DoD Component- and National Archives-approved disposition authorities for CUI are implemented for DoD records and information.

j. Oversees and ensures the Director, DoD Cyber Crime Center:

(1) Manages and updates, as necessary and in coordination with DoD CIO, the policies in Section 236.4 of Title 32, CFR and Section 252.204-7012 of the DFARS.

(2) Maintains the website at https://dibnet.dod.mil to receive contractor mandatory incident reports in accordance with Paragraph 3.9.d(1).

2.10. OSD AND DOD COMPONENT HEADS.

OSD and DoD Component heads:

a. Identify, program, and commit the necessary resources to implement CUI Program requirements as part of their overall information security programs.

b. Designate in writing (with copy to the USD(I&S)):

(1) A DoD Component senior agency official (CSAO) at the Senior Executive Service level or equivalent to implement their CUI Program and perform the duties in Paragraph 3.5.

(2) A DoD Component program manager (CPM) to manage their CUI Program.

c. Ensure their subordinate organizations comply with DoD CUI Program requirements.

d. Ensure their personnel receive initial and annual refresher CUI education and training, and maintain documentation of this training for audit purposes.

e. Report DoD Component training completion data to the USD(I&S) annually or as directed.

f. Provide an annual report to the USD(I&S) on CUI implementation status in accordance with Title 32, CFR, Part 2002.

g. Determine if any CUI documents or materials constitute permanently valuable records of the government, which require maintenance and disposal in accordance with DoDI 5015.02.

h. As the requiring activity, oversee CUI requirements for contractor implementation in partnership with the Defense Contract Management Agency, based on Defense Contract Management Agency responsibilities, or DCSA for cleared contractors in accordance with the NISP, as appropriate.

i. Ensure DoD Component- and National Archives-approved disposition authorities are implemented for DoD records and information regardless of classification.

j. Manage their CUI programs in accordance with guidelines prescribed in this DoD issuance.

2.11. SECRETARIES OF THE MILITARY DEPARTMENTS.

In addition to the responsibilities in Paragraph 2.10., the Secretaries of the Military Departments oversee the implementation of their CUI programs.

2.12. CHAIRMAN OF THE JOINT CHIEFS OF STAFF.

In addition to the responsibilities in Paragraph 2.10., the Chairman of the Joint Chiefs of Staff oversees the implementation of the CUI programs in the Joint Staff organizations and Combatant Commands.

SECTION 3: PROGRAMMATICS

3.1. BACKGROUND.

The CUI EA at NARA, through the Information Security and Oversight Office (ISOO), published and released Part 2002 of Title 32, CFR, which provides implementing requirements for E.O. 13556.

a. Part 2002 of Title 32, CFR established a CUI EA office under NARA's ISOO for implementing and overseeing the CUI Program.

b. Designed as a response to the information sharing challenges from inconsistent definitions and marking requirements applied to CUI, Part 2002 of Title 32 CFR standardized the definition of CUI and codified the identification, sharing, safeguarding, marking, storage, distribution, transmission, decontrol, destruction, training, monitoring, and reporting requirements across the Executive branch of government.

c. In accordance with Part 2002 of Title 32, CFR, CUI requires safeguarding or dissemination controls identified in a law, regulation, or government-wide policy for information that does not meet the requirements for classification in accordance with E.O. 13526.

d. Unlike classified information, an individual or organization generally does not need to demonstrate a need-to-know to access CUI, unless required by a law, regulation, or government-wide policy, but must have a lawful governmental purpose for such access. One example of a requirement for need-to-know established by law, regulation, or government-wide policy is Section 223.6 of Title 32, CFR, which requires a person to have a need-to-know to be granted access to DoD Unclassified Nuclear Information (UCNI).

3.2. LEGACY INFORMATION REQUIREMENTS.

This legacy information guidance applies to information contained across DoD in, among other documents, security classification guides (SCGs), various policies, and other legacy materials falling under the Science and Technology Information Program (DoDI 3200.12), in either electronic or hardcopy format. The CUI Program does not require the redacting or re-marking of documents bearing legacy markings. However, any new document created with information derived from legacy material must be marked as CUI if the information qualifies as CUI.

a. DoD legacy material will not be required to be re-marked or redacted while it remains under DoD control or is accessed online and downloaded for use within the DoD. However, any such document or new derivative document must be marked as CUI if the information qualifies as CUI and the document is being shared outside DoD. DoD legacy marked information stored on a DoD access-controlled website or database does not need to be remarked as CUI, even if other agencies and contractors are granted access to such websites or databases.

b. DoD legacy information does not automatically become CUI. It must be reviewed by the owner of the information to determine if it meets the CUI requirements. If it is determined the specific legacy information meets the CUI requirements, it will be marked in accordance with this issuance and corresponding manual.

c. For federal systems, IS storing information identified as CUI must meet the minimum network security standard in Part 2002 of Title 32, CFR. For nonfederal systems, IS must meet the standards in the NIST SP 800-171, when established by contract.

d. When DoD legacy information is incorporated into, or cited in, another document or material, it must be reviewed for CUI and marked in accordance with this issuance.

3.3. HANDLING REQUIREMENTS.

The DoD CUI Information Security Program will promote, to the maximum extent possible, information sharing, facilitate informed resource use, and simplify its management and implementation while maintaining required safeguarding and handling measures.

a. In accordance with DoDI 5230.09 and the August 14, 2014 Deputy Secretary of Defense Memorandum:

(1) The DoD originator or authorized CUI holder must ensure a prepublication and security policy review is conducted, pursuant to the standard DoD Component process, before CUI is approved for public release, which includes publication to a publicly accessible website.

(2) Decontrolling and releasing CUI records will be executed by the originator of the information, the original classification authority (OCA) if identified in a security classification guide, or designated offices for decontrolling CUI pursuant to the procedures for the review and release of information under the FOIA in accordance with the November 19, 2018 ISOO Notice. There are no specific timelines to decontrol CUI unless specifically required in a law, regulation, or government-wide policy. Decontrol will occur when the CUI no longer requires safeguarding and will follow DoD records management procedures.

b. OCAs will determine if aggregated CUI under their control should be classified in accordance with Volume 1 of DoDM 5200.01 and will confirm the relevant SCGs address the compilation.

c. DoD information systems processing, storing, or transmitting CUI will be categorized at the "moderate" confidentiality impact level and follow the guidance in DoDIs 8500.01 and 8510.01. Non-DoD information systems processing, storing, or transmitting CUI will provide adequate security, and the appropriate requirements must be incorporated into all contracts, grants, and other legal agreements with non-DoD entities in accordance with DoDI 8582.01. See Section 5 of this issuance for more information on CUI and its application to industry.

d. The DoD CUI Registry provides an official list of the Indexes and Categories used to identify the various types of DoD CUI. The DoD CUI Registry mirrors the National CUI Registry, but provides additional information on the relationships to DoD by aligning each Index and Category to DoD issuances.

(1) The official DoD CUI Registry of categories can be accessed on Intelink at https://intelshare.intelink.gov/sites/ousdi/hcis/sec/icdirect/information/CUI/Forms/AllItems.aspx

(2) The site will be updated as changes to the DoD CUI Registry are made based on official notification from the CUI EA through the CUI Registry Working Group; changes to law, regulation, or government-wide policy; or notification that the information no longer meets the requirements for CUI.

3.4. MARKING REQUIREMENTS.

This paragraph covers the essential marking requirements for initial phased implementation of the DoD CUI Program.

a. At minimum, CUI markings for unclassified DoD documents will include the acronym "CUI" in the banner and footer of the document.

b. If portion markings are selected, then all document subjects and titles, as well as individual sections, parts, paragraphs, or similar portions of a CUI document known to contain CUI, will be portion marked with "(CUI)." Use of the unclassified marking "(U)" as a portion marking for unclassified information within CUI documents or materials is required.

(1) There is no requirement to add the "U," signifying unclassified, to the banner and footer as was required with the old FOUO marking (i.e., U//FOUO).

(2) Banners, footers, and portion marking will only be marked "Unclassified" or "(U)" for unclassified information in accordance with the June 4, 2019 ISOO letter. If the document also contains CUI, it will be marked in accordance with Paragraph 3.4.a. and additional forthcoming guidance.

c. CUI markings in classified documents will appear in paragraphs or subparagraphs known to contain **only** CUI and must be portion marked with "(CUI)." "CUI" will **not** appear in the banner or footer.

(1) There will be an acknowledgement added to the warning box on the first page of multi-page documents to alert readers to the presence of CUI in a classified DoD document, as shown in Figure 1.

Figure 1. CUI Warning Box for Classified Material

This content is classified at the [insert highest classification level of the source data] level and may contain elements of controlled unclassified information (CUI), unclassified, or information classified at a lower level than the overall classification displayed. This content shall not be used as a source of derivative classification; refer instead to [cite specific reference, where possible, or state "the applicable classification guide(s)"]. It must be reviewed for both Classified National Security Information (CNSI) and CUI in accordance with DoDI 5230.09 prior to public release. [Add a point of contact when needed.]

(2) Volume 2 of DoDM 5200.01 requires DoD intelligence producers to follow DNI formats for intelligence production under the authority of the DNI. When DoD CUI is ncorporated into a Digital Access Policy under the authority of the DNI, the information and the document will follow the Digital Access Policy standards established by the DNI.

d. The dissemination marking "not releasable to foreign nationals (NOFORN or NF)" is an ntelligence control marking used to identify intelligence information an originator has determined meets the criteria of Intelligence Community Directive 710 and Intelligence Community Policy Guidance 403.1, which provides guidance for further dissemination control narkings. It must be applied to controlled unclassified intelligence information that is properly characterized as CUI with appropriate CUI markings. CUI identified with this marking will not be provided, in any form, to foreign governments (including coalition partners), international organizations, foreign nationals, or other non-U.S. persons without the originator's approval in accordance with E.O.s 13526 and 13556. If originator approval is required for further dissemination, the originator will mark the requirement on the information in accordance with Section 4.1(i)(1) of E.O. 13526.

(1) The application of the control marking "not releasable to foreign nationals" NOFORN or NF) will only be applied, when warranted, to unclassified intelligence information properly categorized as CUI and reviewed by a Foreign Disclosure Officer to ensure there are no nternational agreements in place to prohibit its use and prohibiting sharing.

(2) The control marking NOFORN or NF will be applied to Naval Nuclear Propulsion nformation (NNPI), Unclassified Controlled Nuclear Information (UCNI), National Disclosure Policy (NDP-1), and cover and cover support information. When warranted, it can be applied to unclassified information properly categorized as CUI having a licensing or export control requirement. Before marking a document or material as NOFORN or NF, it will be reviewed by he Foreign Disclosure Officer to ensure there are no agreements in place to prohibit its use and sharing.

(3) The application of "Releasable to" ("REL TO") can only be applied, when warranted and consistent with relevant law, regulation, or government-wide policy or DoD policy, to nformation properly categorized as CUI with an export control or licensing requirement with a foreign disclosure agreement in place.

(a) Export-controlled CUI transfers to foreign persons must be in accordance with the Arms Export Control Act, International Traffic in Arms Regulations, Export Control Reform Act, Export Administration Regulations, and DoDI 2040.02. In accordance with DoDDs 5230.11 and 5230.20, a positive foreign disclosure decision must be made before CUI is released to a foreign entity.

(b) DoD operational CUI (not related to intelligence) may be marked as REL TO.

e. All classified documents, including legacy documents will be reviewed for CUI and properly marked upon changes in the document's classification level, particularly if the documents are to be completely declassified.

f. The first page or cover of any document or material containing CUI, including a document with commingled classified information, will include a CUI designation indicator, as shown in Figure 2. This CUI designation indicator is similar to the classification-marking block used for CNSI documents and materials. Documents and materials containing CUI will require a generic "CUI" marking at the top and bottom of each page.

(1) In accordance with Part 2002 of Title 32, CFR, the CUI designation indicator must contain, at minimum, the name of the DoD Component determining that the information is CUI. If letterhead or another standard indicator of origination is used, this line may be omitted.

(2) The second line must identify the office making the determination.

(3) The third line must identify all types of CUI contained in the document.

(4) The fourth line must contain the distribution statement or the dissemination controls applicable to the document.

(5) The fifth line must contain the phone number or office mailbox for the originating DoD Component or authorized CUI holder.

Figure 2. CUI Designation Indicator for All Documents and Material

Controlled by: [Name of DoD Component] (Only if not on letterhead)
Controlled by: [Name of Office]
CUI Category: (List category or categories of CUI)
Distribution/Dissemination Control:
POC: [Phone or email address]

g. During DoD's initial phased implementation of the CUI Program, there is no required distinction that must be made between Basic and Specified CUI. All DoD information will be protected in accordance with the requirements under the Basic level of safeguards and dissemination unless specifically identified otherwise in a law, regulation, or government-wide policy. Forthcoming guidance will address the distinction between the two levels of CUI, including a list of which categories are Basic or Specified, what makes the category one or the other, and the unique requirements, to include markings, for each.

3.5. GENERAL DOD CUI ADMINISTRATIVE REQUIREMENTS.

Each DoD Component head must appoint, in writing, a CSAO for the Information Security Program, who will:

a. Appoint, in writing, an official to serve as the CPM for CUI in accordance with ISSO Notice 2019-02. To manage the DoD Component's overall execution of the CUI program, the CPM will:

(1) Coordinate directly with the USD(I&S) Information Security Directorate on CUI matters.

(2) Manage and oversee CUI implementation for the DoD Component.

(3) Inform the CSAO of concerns identified by subordinate elements.

(4) Report misuse, mishandling, or UD of CUI to the Unauthorized Disclosure Program Management Office. In addition, notify the appropriate Military Department Counterintelligence Organization of all incidents.

(5) Submit the annual CUI Implementation Status Report to the DDI(CL&S) to evaluate the effectiveness, compliance, and efficiency of the DoD Component's implementation of CUI, in accordance with Paragraph 3.6.c.

(6) Resolve CUI challenges in accordance with E.O. 13556 and Part 2002 of Title 32, CFR. Refer all unresolved challenges to the DDI(CL&S).

b. Serve as the primary point of contact for official correspondence, accountability reporting, and other matters of record between the DoD Component and the USD(I&S).

3.6. GENERAL DOD CUI PROCEDURES.

DoD CUI is clustered into organizational indexes (e.g., defense, privacy, proprietary) with associated categories, and is categorized by the DoD according to the specific law, regulation, or government-wide policy requiring control. Unclassified information associated with a law, regulation, or government-wide policy and identified as needing safeguarding is considered CUI. It requires access control, handling, marking, dissemination controls, and other protective measures for safeguarding.

a. The authorized holder of a document or material is responsible for determining, at the time of creation, whether information in a document or material falls into a CUI category. If so, the authorized holder is responsible for applying CUI markings and dissemination instructions accordingly.

b. In accordance with this issuance, every individual at every level, including DoD civilian and military personnel as well as contractors providing support to the DoD pursuant to contractual requirements, will comply with the requirements in Paragraph 3.6.f of this issuance for initial and annual refresher CUI training.

c. Each OSD and DoD Component will annually submit the CUI Implementation Status Report to the USD(I&S) for inclusion in the DoD CUI Program report to the CUI EA. A copy of the report will be made available on Intelink at https://intelshare.intelink.gov/sites/ousdi/hcis/sec/icdirect/information/CUI/Forms/AllItems.aspx. The CUI Implementation Status Report will at least include:

(1) Implementation activities.

(2) Training statistics.

(3) Incident management.

(4) Implementation and sustainment costs.

(5) Self-inspection activities.

d. DoD and OSD Components will submit an initial report on the implementation status of their CUI Programs. Once established, DoD Component heads will conduct inspections of their programs, and the DoD Implementation Status Report will transition to an annual self-inspection report.

e. Some documents and materials containing CUI may constitute permanently valuable government records and will be maintained and disposed of in accordance with the NARA-approved record disposition schedules applicable to each DoD Component in accordance with DoDI 5015.02. When other materials containing CUI no longer require safeguarding, they will be decontrolled and either retained, if a permanent record, or destroyed in accordance with Section 4 and ISOO Notice 2019-03.

f. Other Executive Branch Agencies in the U.S. Government have identified organizational indexes and CUI categories related to a law, regulation, or government-wide policy. Some CUI indexes and categories are unique to specific organizations. The Official CUI Registry is on the NARA Website at https://www.archives.gov/cui. It identifies other CUI categories not specific to the Defense Index, but that may apply or relate to the Executive Branch. Since various DoD Components interact and share inter-dependencies with other departments, agencies, and activities in the Executive Branch, it is important to know and understand these indexes and categories, along with their associated markings, in order to recognize other agencies' CUI and handle the information accordingly. Of note, the CUI indexes and categories listed in the CUI Registry and DoD CUI Registry identify the safeguarding and dissemination requirements as identified by the related law, regulation, or government-wide policy. Moreover, the CUI Registry is agile and subject to change based on changes in law, regulation, or government-wide policy.

g. In accordance with ISOO Notice 2016-01, CUI training standards must, at minimum:

(1) Identify individual responsibilities for protecting CUI.

(2) Identify the organizational index with CUI categories routinely handled by DoD personnel.

(3) Describe the CUI Registry, including purpose, structure, and location (http://www.archives.gov/cui).

(4) Describe the differences between CUI Basic and CUI Specified.

(5) Identify the offices or organizations with DoD CUI Program oversight responsibilities.

(6) Address CUI marking requirements as described in this issuance.

(7) Address the required physical safeguards and CUI protection methods as described in this issuance.

(8) Address the destruction requirements and methods as described in this issuance.

(9) Address the incident reporting procedures as described in this issuance.

(10) Address methods for properly disseminating CUI within the DoD and with external entities inside and outside of the Executive Branch.

(11) Address the methods for properly decontrolling CUI as described in this issuance.

3.7. GENERAL DOD CUI REQUIREMENTS.

This section specifies initial requirements for implementing, marking, and managing the CUI program. Table 1 contains a sample list of the categories found in the DoD CUI Registry and Defense Index. A complete list of CUI Indexes and Categories can be found on Intelink at https://intelshare.intelink.gov/sites/ousdi/hcis/sec/icdirect/information/CUI/Forms/AllItems.aspx. Some significant points about DoD CUI include:

a. CUI does not include information lawfully and publicly available without restrictions.

b. CUI requires safeguarding measures identified by the CUI EA in Part 2002.14 of Title 32, CFR and, as necessary, in the law, regulation, or government-wide policy with which it is associated. DoD CUI may be disseminated to DoD personnel to conduct official DoD and U.S. Government business in accordance with a law, regulation, or government-wide policy.

(1) No individual may have access to CUI information unless it is determined he or she has an authorized, lawful government purpose.

(2) The person with authorized possession, knowledge, or control of CUI will determine whether an individual has an authorized, lawful government purpose to access designated CUI.

(3) CUI information may be disseminated within the DoD Components and between DoD Component officials and DoD contractors, consultants, and grantees to conduct official

business for the DoD, provided dissemination is consistent with controls imposed by a distribution statement or limited dissemination controls (LDC).

(4) CUI designated information may be disseminated to a foreign recipient in order to conduct official business for the DoD, provided the dissemination has been approved by a disclosure authority in accordance with Paragraph 3.4.c. and the CUI is appropriately marked as releasable to the intended foreign recipient.

c. CTI compiled or aggregated may become classified. Such classified CTI is subject to the requirements of the National Industrial Security Program, which has different requirements than Section 252.204-7012 of the DFARS for unclassified CTI.

(1) CTI is to be marked with one of the Distribution Statements B through F, in accordance with DoDI 5230.24.

(2) Pursuant to section 252.204-7012 of the DFARS, scientific, technical, and engineering information beyond basic research(known as pre-applied research and development aligning with the Science, Technology, and Engineering Information Program policies, with military or space application subject to controls on the access, use, reproduction, modification, performance, transmission, display, release, disclosure, or dissemination) shall be treated as CUI. This type of information or data can become classified by compilation or aggregation and is subject to the National Disclosure Policy (NDP-1). Examples include preliminary research and engineering data, engineering drawings, and associated specifications, lists, standards, process sheets, manuals, technical reports, technical orders, studies and analyses on topics requested by DoD Components, catalog-item identifications, data sets, and computer software with executable or source code.

d. As DoD programs transition through the acquisition life cycle, the CUI category or treatment of information may change. In accordance with Title 32, CFR, if the safeguarding requirements for a CUI category or the original law, regulation, or government-wide policy changes, there will be a cascading effect requiring changes for the particular category. These changes will be implemented as soon as possible.

(1) For example, in the acquisition area, a program will begin in the basic research and development phase. Once this program milestone is achieved, the project could transition to the applied research and development or to the production phase.

(2) At this point, the original CUI must be reviewed for any necessary adjustments, including potential changes to the CUI designation, category, subcategory or type, or controls.

e. CUI will be identified in SCGs to ensure such information receives appropriate protection. If the SCG is canceled, a memorandum or other guidance document may be issued to identify CUI instead.

f. DoD is required to provide documents and records requested by members of the public, unless those records are exempt from disclosure in accordance with the procedures established by Part 286 of Title 32, CFR and DoDD 5400.07.

g. Other CUI category information may qualify for withholding from public release based on a specific FOIA exemption for the type of information in question. Determining whether information meets the requirements for CUI shall be done separately and prior to identifying any potential FOIA exemptions.

h. CUI requiring distribution statements in accordance with DODI 5230.24 or the LDC identified in the related law, regulation, or government-wide policy, but does not qualify as classified information in accordance with E.O. 13526 or Chapter 14 of Title 42, U.S.C, (also known and referred to in this issuance as the "Atomic Energy Act of 1954"), will be implemented in accordance with this issuance.

i. Table 1 is an example of the format for the list of all DoD CUI Registry Categories aligned to the CUI National Registry published on Intelink at https://intelshare.intelink.gov/sites/ousdi/hcis/sec/icdirect/information/CUI/Forms/AllItems.aspx.

j. Table 1 provides a sample of the cross-walk of the National CUI registry to the DoD issuance(s) related to the category. The items in Table 1 identify the two unique types of data used by the Department of Energy, the DoD, and the DoD Components. Both types satisfy the CUI requirements and are subject to safeguarding and limited distribution control, and are exempt from mandatory public disclosure in accordance with Exemption 3 of the FOIA.

Table 1. DoD CUI Registry Category Examples

Category	Proposed Defense Description	Additional Information (How Used, Examples, etc.)	Authority	DoD Guidance	Miscellaneous Information
NNPI	Related to the safety of reactors and associated naval nuclear propulsion plants, and control of radiation and radioactivity associated with naval nuclear propulsion activities, including prescribing and enforcing standards and regulations for these areas as they affect the environment and the safety and health of workers, operators, and the general public. This subcategory of Defense CUI relates to the protection of information concerning nuclear reactors, materials, or security and concerns the safeguarding of nuclear reactors, materials, or security. Refer to Office of the Chief of Naval Operations Instruction N9210.3, and CG-RN-1, Revision 3, Department of Energy-DoD Classification Guide for the Naval Nuclear Propulsion Program for guidance on determining information as Unclassified Defense-NNPI.	Data and information related to the safety of reactors and associated naval nuclear propulsion plants, the control of radiation and radioactivity associated with Defense naval nuclear propulsion activities containing prescriptive and enforcement standards and regulations for these areas as they affect the environment and the safety and health of workers, operators, and the general public.	Section 2013 of Title 42, U.S.C.; Section 2511 of Title 50, U.S.C.	Chief of Naval Operations Instruction N9210.3, and CG-RN-1, Revision 3.	Sanctions: Section 2168 and 2168(b) of Title 42, U.S.C. **The DoD NNPI is unique as it is exempt from mandatory public disclosure under Exemption 3 of the FOIA.**
Unclassified Controlled Nuclear Information - Defense	Relating to Department of Defense special nuclear material (SNM), equipment, and facilities, as defined by Part 223 of Title 32, CFR. This type of Defense CUI is unclassified information about SNM security measures, DoD SNM equipment, DoD SNM facilities, or nuclear weapons in DoD custody. Information is designated DoD unclassified controlled nuclear information (UCNI) in accordance with DoDI 5210.83 only when it is determined its UD could reasonably be expected to have a significant adverse effect on the health and safety of the public or the common defense and security by significantly increasing the likelihood of the illegal production of nuclear weapons or the theft, diversion, or sabotage of DoD SNM, DoD SNM equipment, DoD SNM facilities, or nuclear weapons in DoD custody.	This type of Defense CUI may be designated UCNI by the Heads of the DoD Components and individuals delegated authority in accordance with DoDD 5210.83. Some specific examples include: Security plans, procedures, and equipment used for the physical safeguarding of DoD SNM.	Section 128(a) of Title 10, U.S.C.; Part 223 of Title 32, CFR	DoDD 5210.83; DoDI 5210.83;	**The DoD UCNI is unique as it is exempt from mandatory public disclosure under Exemption 3 of the FOIA.**

k. Restricted data or formerly restricted data are classified and shall not be commingled with CUI in an unclassified document. For restricted data or formerly restricted data, follow the marking requirements in accordance with Volume 2 of DoDM 5200.01; Part 1045 of Title 10, CFR; and the Atomic Energy Act of 1954.

l. For DoD Geospatial intelligence information and data, the DoD will not apply the Geodetic Product Information (GPI) designation. Instead, the DoD will continue to use the designation for "Limited Distribution" with the marking of "LIMDIS." For all other DoD geospatial information and data, such as installation geospatial information and services (IGI&S) as defined by DoDI 8130.01, use the GPI category or other appropriate CUI category designations defined by this issuance. The DoD will use the GPI designation for all of the non-Geospatial intelligence information and data. Approved LDCs for the DoD are located on Intelink at https://intelshare.intelink.gov/sites/ousdi/hcis/sec/icdirect/information/CUI/Forms/AllItems.aspx.

m. The request for a waiver for a particular CUI Program requirement will be handled in accordance with Volume 1 of DoDM 5200.01 for CNSI.

n. DoD Component heads shall produce annual self-inspection reports and general program status updates to fulfill ISOO monitoring and reporting requirements.

3.8. OCA.

DoD OCAs will determine if CUI under their control, when compiled, is classified. If so, the applicable SCGs must address the compilation. Any time an OCA discovers that compiled or aggregated information is not properly classified on websites, folders, or documents, the OCA will:

a. Notify the organization using the compiled information to remove or protect the information.

b. Conduct a damage assessment.

c. Determine if the information still requires classified protection in its compiled form. If not, the OCA must document the revised aggregation or compilation determination by updating SCGs and providing the guide to all users in accordance with DoDM 5200.45.

d. If the information is determined not to be classified, it must be reviewed to identify if the information is CUI.

e. Since OCAs are the owners of the information under their authority, they are authorized to identify and mark such information as CUI.

3.9. GENERAL RELEASE AND DISCLOSURE REQUIREMENTS.

a. The release or disclosure to foreign governments, international organizations, coalitions, or allied personnel of CUI not controlled as NOFORN will be in accordance with a law, regulation, or government-wide policy. Access to such CUI during official foreign national visits and assignments to DoD Components and cleared contractor facilities, when applied by contract, will be in accordance with DoDD 5230.20.

b. CUI not controlled as NOFORN may be released or disclosed to non-U.S. citizens employed by the DoD if:

(1) Access to such information is within the scope of their assigned duties.

(2) Access to such information would help accomplish a lawful and authorized DoD mission or purpose and would not be detrimental to the interests of the DoD or the U.S. Government.

(3) There are no contract restrictions prohibiting access to such information.

(4) Access to such information is in accordance with DoDIs 8500.01 and 5200.02 and export control regulations, as applicable.

c. The DoD Components' CSAOs and CPMs will establish procedures to ensure prompt and appropriate management action is taken in cases of CUI misuse, including UD of CUI, improper CUI designation and marking, violation of this issuance, and incidents potentially placing CUI at risk of UD. Such actions will focus on correcting or eliminating the conditions contributing to the incident.

d. For UD of CUI, no formal security inquiry or investigation is required unless disciplinary action will be taken against the individual(s) responsible. In such cases, a preliminary inquiry is appropriate. UD of certain CUI, such as export controlled-technical data, may also result in potential civil and criminal sanctions against responsible persons based on the procedures codified in the relevant law, regulation, or government-wide policy. The DoD Component originating the CUI will be informed of any UD.

e. Reporting or accounting for UD of CUI shall be done in accordance with Paragraph 3.5.a(4), and the appropriate Military Department Counterintelligence Organization shall be notified of all incidents.

3.10. GENERAL SYSTEM AND NETWORK CUI REQUIREMENTS.

In accordance with DoDIs 8500.01 and 8510.01, security controls for systems and networks are set to the level required by the safeguarding requirements for the data or information being processed, as identified in Federal Information Processing Standards 199 and 200. For DoD CUI, the minimum security level will be moderate confidentiality in accordance with Part 2002 of Title 32, CFR and NIST SP 800-171.

a. The USD(I&S) will notify and coordinate with the CUI EA regarding waiver requests involving CUI requirements prior to granting any such requests, including waiver requests elated to IS. The USD(I&S) must coordinate and collaborate with the DoD CIO to ensure the gency requesting the waiver has plans to appropriately safeguard and control CUI. The request or a waiver for a CUI Program requirement shall be done in accordance with Volume 1 of DoDM 5200.01 for CNSI, as modified in the forthcoming manual supporting this instruction.

b. DoD personnel will not use unofficial or personal (e.g., .net; .com) e-mail accounts, nessaging systems, or other non-DoD information systems, except approved or authorized government contractor systems, to conduct official business involving CUI. This is necessary to nsure proper accountability for Federal records and to facilitate data spill remediation in ccordance with Public Law 113-187 and the January 16, 2018 Deputy Secretary of Defense nemorandum.

c. DoD information systems processing, storing, or transmitting CUI will be categorized at he moderate impact level, and follow the guidance in DoDIs 8500.01 and 8510.01. Non-DoD nformation systems processing, storing, or transmitting CUI will provide adequate security, and he appropriate requirements must be incorporated into all contacts, grants, and other legal greements with non-DoD entities in accordance with DoDI 8582.01. The NIST SP 800-171 governs and protects CUI on non-Federal IS when applied by contract.

d. For systems, networks, and programs operating on the various domains, a splash screen varning and notice of consent, as shown in Figure 3, must be employed to alert users of CUI vithin the program. This ensures proper safeguarding and dissemination controls are mplemented in accordance with Part 2002 of Title 32, CFR and this issuance.

Figure 3. Notice and Consent

"You are accessing a U.S. Government (USG) Information System (IS) that is provided for USG-authorized use only. By using this IS (which includes any device attached to this IS), you consent to the following conditions:

-The USG routinely intercepts and monitors communications on this IS for purposes including, but not limited to, penetration testing, COMSEC monitoring, network operations and defense, personnel misconduct (PM), law enforcement (LE), and counterintelligence (CI) investigations.

-At any time, the USG may inspect and seize data stored on this IS.

-Communications using, or data stored on, this IS are not private, are subject to routine monitoring, interception, and search, and may be disclosed or used for any USG-authorized purpose.

-This IS includes security measures (e.g., authentication and access controls) to protect USG interests--not for your personal benefit or privacy.

-Notwithstanding the above, using this IS does not constitute consent to PM, LE or CI investigative searching or monitoring of the content of privileged communications, or work product, related to personal representation or services by attorneys, psychotherapists, or clergy, and their assistants. Such communications and work product are private and confidential. See User Agreement for details."

e. Organizations will modify or install classification marking tools on UNCLASSIFIED, SECRET, and TOP SECRET network systems to account for CUI information and readily permit inclusion of CUI markings and designator indicators as required by Part 2002 of Title 32, CFR.

SECTION 4: DISSEMINATION, DECONTROLLING, AND DESTRUCTION OF CUI

4.1. GENERAL.

Part 2002 of Title 32, CFR requires dissemination statements to be placed on classified and unclassified documents or other materials when CUI necessitates access restrictions, including those required by law, regulation, or government-wide policy. These statements facilitate control, secondary sharing, decontrol, and release without the need to repeatedly obtain approval or authorization from the controlling DoD office.

a. Dissemination controls identify the audience deemed to have a lawful government purpose to use the CUI and specify the rationale for applying the controls by specific codes in accordance with DoDI 5230.24 and this issuance.

b. Agencies must promptly decontrol CUI properly determined by the CUI owner to no longer require safeguarding or dissemination controls, unless doing so conflicts with the related law, regulation, or government-wide policy in accordance with DoDI 5230.09.

c. Decontrolling CUI through the public release process relieves authorized holders from requirements for handling information in accordance with the CUI Program. A prepublication review must be conducted in accordance with DoDI 5230.09 before public release may be authorized.

d. In accordance with Part 2002.20 of Title 32, CFR, if the authorized holder of the CUI publicly releases the CUI in accordance with the designating agency's authorized procedures, this constitutes the decontrol of the document.

e. To ensure CUI protection, the following measures will be implemented:

(1) During working hours, steps will be taken to minimize the risk of access by unauthorized personnel, such as not reading, discussing, or leaving CUI information unattended where unauthorized personnel are present. After working hours, CUI information will be stored in unlocked containers, desks, or cabinets if the government or government-contract building provides security for continuous monitoring of access. If building security is not provided, the information will be stored in locked desks, file cabinets, bookcases, locked rooms, or similarly secured areas. The concept of a controlled environment means there is sufficient internal security measures in place to prevent or detect unauthorized access to CUI. For DoD, an open storage environment meets these requirements.

(2) CUI information and material may be transmitted via first class mail, parcel post, or, bulk shipments. When practical, CUI information may be transmitted electronically (e.g., data, website, or e-mail), via approved secure communications systems or systems utilizing other protective measures such as Public Key Infrastructure or transport layer security (e.g., https). Avoid wireless telephone transmission of CUI when other options are available. CUI transmission via facsimile machine is permitted; however, the sender is responsible for

determining whether appropriate protection will be available at the receiving location before transmission (e.g., facsimile machine attended by a person authorized to receive CUI; facsimile machine located in a controlled government environment).

4.2. DISSEMINATION REQUIREMENTS FOR DOD CUI.

a. In accordance with this issuance, CUI access should be encouraged and permitted to the extent the access or dissemination:

(1) Complies with the law, regulation, or government-wide policy identifying the information as CUI.

(2) Furthers a lawful government purpose.

(3) Is not restricted by an authorized LDC established by the CUI EA.

(4) Is not otherwise prohibited by any other law, regulation, or government-wide policy.

b. Agencies may place limits on disseminating CUI for a lawful government purpose only using the dissemination controls listed in Table 2 or methods authorized by a specific law, regulation, or government-wide policy.

c. When handling other Executive Branch CUI, DoD personnel will follow their governance criteria for when the application of dissemination controls and its markings are allowed, and by whom, while ensuring the policy is in accordance with Part 2002 of Title 32, CFR.

d. LDCs or distribution statements cannot unnecessarily restrict CUI access.

e. Since DoD Components need to retain certain agency-specific CUI within their organizations, DoD Components may use the limited dissemination controls to limit access to those on an accompanying dissemination list, as shown in Table 2. For example, raw data, information, or products must be processed and analyzed before determining if further dissemination is required or permitted. The Limited Dissemination Control List control will be used to address this need. The LDC list is found on Intelink at https://intelshare.intelink.gov/sites/ousdi/hcis/sec/icdirect/information/CUI/Forms/AllItems.aspx

4.3. LEGACY DISTRIBUTION STATEMENTS.

a. Legacy CUI technical documents and materials requiring export control have used distribution statements in accordance with DoDI 5230.24 in order to address the shared responsibility between the DoD and its contractors to safeguard this information. This was done for legacy CUI creation, transmission, receipt, storage, distribution, decontrol, and approved disposition authorities, including destruction.

b. As of the effective date of this issuance, DoD personnel will use LDCs for new CUI documents and materials except export controlled technical information, which must be marked with an export control warning in accordance with DoDI 5230.24, DoDD 5230.25, and Part 250 of Title 32, CFR. The wording of the distribution statements may not be modified to specify additional distribution, such as distribution to foreign governments. However, where other markings are authorized and used in accordance with associated law, regulation, or government-wide policy (e.g., North Atlantic Treaty Organization markings, REL TO), those markings may be used to further inform distribution decisions. Therefore, "REL TO" is authorized for use with foreign nationals once the information distribution is properly coordinated with the foreign disclosure office.

Table 2. Dissemination Control and Distribution Statement Markings

NEW LDC	ALIGNMENT TO CURRENT
NONE – Publicly Releasable **AFTER** Review	DISTRO A
No Foreign Dissemination (NOFORN / NF)	
Federal Employees Only (FED ONLY)	DISTRO B
Federal Employees and Contractors Only (FEDCON)	DISTRO C
No Dissemination to Contractors (NOCON)	
Dissemination List Controlled (DL ONLY)	DISTRO F
Authorized for Release to Certain Foreign Nationals Only (REL TO USA, LIST)	
Display Only (DISPLAY ONLY)	
Dissemination List – (Include Separate List for Government Only)*	DISTRO E
Dissemination List – (Include Separate List for Government and Contractors Only)*	DISTRO D
NONE	DISTRO X: U.S. Government Agencies and private individuals or enterprises eligible to obtain export controlled technical data in accordance with DoDD 5230.25. DISTRO X was cancelled and superseded by DISTRO C.
*The dissemination list limits access to the specified individuals, groups, or agencies and must accompany the document	

c. CUI export controlled technical information or other scientific, technical, and engineering information will still use distribution statements. Export controlled information must also be marked with an export control warning as directed in DoDI 5230.24, DoDD 5230.25, and Part 250 of Title 32, CFR.

4.4. DECONTROLLING.

Guidance for decontrolling CUI records, documents, and materials is provided in this issuance, or the CUI Registry for information categories not directly related to DoD CUI.

a. CUI documents and materials will be formally reviewed in accordance with DoDI 5230.09 before being decontrolled or released to the public.

b. The originator or other competent authority (e.g., initial FOIA denial and appellate authorities) will terminate the CUI status of specific information when the information no longer requires protection from public disclosure. When the CUI status of information is terminated in this manner, all known holders will be notified by email or other means. Upon notification, holders will remove the CUI markings. Holders will not need to retrieve records on file solely for this purpose. Information with a terminated CUI status will not be publicly released without review and approval in accordance with DoDIs 5230.09, 5230.29, and 5400.04.

4.5. DESTRUCTION.

Guidance for destroying CUI documents and materials is provided in this issuance, the CUI Registry, and ISOO Notice 2019-03. CUI documents and materials will be formally reviewed in accordance with Paragraphs 4.5.a. and 4.5.b. before approved disposition authorities are applied, including destruction. Media containing CUI must include decontrolling indicators.

a. Record and non-record copies of CUI documents will be disposed of in accordance with Chapter 33 of Title 44, U.S.C. and the DoD Components' records management directives. When destroying CUI, including in electronic form, agencies must do so in a manner making it unreadable, indecipherable, and irrecoverable. If the law, regulation, or government-wide policy specifies a method of destruction, agencies must use the method prescribed.

b. Record and non-record CUI documents may be destroyed by means approved for destroying classified information or by any other means making it unreadable, indecipherable, and unrecoverable the original information such as those identified in NIST SP 800-88 and in accordance with Section 2002.14 of Title 32, CFR.

SECTION 5: APPLICATION OF DOD INDUSTRY

5.1. GENERAL.

There is a shared responsibility between the DoD and industry, when established by contract, grants, or other legal agreements or arrangements, in the identification, creation, sharing, marking, safeguarding, storage, dissemination, decontrol, disposition, destruction, and records management of CUI documents and materials. It is essential to identify and apply the general dissemination principles and guidance as prescribed by the CUI EA in accordance with Part 2002 of Title 32, CFR. Contracts containing CUI shared from DoD or generated, managed, or transmitted by the contractor via their information systems, will be in accordance with this issuance, which will be incorporated into each DoD contract.

a. The NIST SP 800-171 identifies the baseline CUI system security requirements for industry established by Part 2002 of Title 32, CFR. Additionally, Section 252.204-7012 of the DFARS specifies a waiver process for defense contractors in accordance with NIST SP 800-171 for contractor IT or networks.

b. CUI with the potential to impact national security (e.g., information related to critical programs and technology information) may require enhanced protection. These enhanced measures would address both physical and logical procedures. Enhanced protection methods for systems hosting CUI include:

(1) Access control (e.g., restricting both physical and logical access to the systems).

(2) Audit and accountability (e.g., review and monitor system usage).

(3) Configuration management (e.g., restrict system connection to only approved resources).

(4) Identification and authentication (e.g., control issuance of end-user certificates).

(5) Incident response (e.g., ensure corrective measures are implemented in a timely manner and validate effectiveness).

(6) System and communication protection (e.g., application of encryption for data at rest and restriction of connections to uncertified, unsecured, non-organizational systems). DoD Components may implement stricter CUI encryption requirements based on a law, regulation, or government-wide policy (DHA PI 8140, requires workforce encrypt emailed PHI).

(7) System and information integrity (e.g., provide network detection tools throughout the system to identify attempted intrusions).

c. Non-DoD IS processing, storing, or transmitting CUI will be safeguarded in accordance with contractual requirements identified for the particular CUI contained in the contract, DoDI 8582.01 and Section 252.204-7012 of the DFARS or their subsequent revisions.

d. When established by contract, contractors, sub-contractors, and consultants must comply with safeguarding requirements identified in the contract for all types of CUI.

e. The program office or requiring activity must identify DoD CUI at the time of contract award and, if necessary, provide guidance on information aggregation or compilation. The program office or requiring activity must review recurring or renewed contracts for CUI to comply with this issuance.

5.2. MISUSE OR UD OF CUI.

Safeguarding requirements and incident response measures for misuse or UD of CUI must be implemented across the DoD. Senior leaders, contracting officers, commanders, and supervisors at all levels must consider and take appropriate administrative, legal, or other corrective or disciplinary action to address CUI misuse or UD commensurate with the appropriate law, regulation, or government-wide policy.

5.3. REQUIREMENTS FOR DOD CONTRACTORS.

This paragraph highlights requirements for DoD contractors.

a. Whenever DoD provides information to contractors, it must identify whether any of the information is CUI via the contracting vehicle, in whole or part, and mark such documents, material, or media in accordance with this issuance.

b. Whenever the DoD provides CUI to, or CUI is generated by, non-DoD entities, protective measures and dissemination controls, including those directed by relevant law, regulation, or government-wide policy, will be articulated in the contract, grant, or other legal agreement, as appropriate.

c. DoD contracts must require contractors to monitor CUI for aggregation and compilation based on the potential to generate classified information pursuant to security classification guidance addressing the accumulation of unclassified data or information. DoD contracts shall require contractors to report the potential classification of aggregated or compiled CUI to a DoD representative.

d. DoD personnel and contractors, pursuant to mandatory DoD contract provisions, will submit unclassified DoD information for review and approval for release in accordance with the standard DoD Component processes and DoDI 5230.09.

e. All CUI records must follow the approved mandatory disposition authorities whenever the DoD provides CUI to, or CUI is generated by, non-DoD entities in accordance with Section 1220-1236 of Title 36, CFR, Section 3301a of Title 44, U.S.C., and this issuance.

GLOSSARY

G.1. ACRONYMS.

ACRONYM	MEANING
CFR	Code of Federal Regulations
CMO	Chief Management Officer of the Department of Defense
CNSI	classified national security information
CPM	Component program manager
CSAO	Component senior agency official
CTI	controlled technical information
CUI	controlled unclassified information
DDI(CL&S)	Director For Defense Intelligence (Counterintelligence, Law Enforcement, And Security)
DCSA	Defense Counterintelligence and Security Agency
DFARS	Defense Federal Acquisition Regulation Supplement
DNI	Director of National Intelligence
DoD CIO	Department of Defense Chief Information Officer
DoDD	DoD directive
DoDI	DoD instruction
DoDM	DoD manual
EA	Executive Agent
E.O.	Executive order
FOIA	Freedom of Information Act
GPI	Geodetic Product Information
ISOO	Information Security Oversight Office
IS	information systems
LDC	limited dissemination controls
NARA	National Archives and Records Administration
NISP	National Industrial Security Program
NIST SP	National Institute of Standards and Technology Special Publication
NNPI	Naval Nuclear Propulsion Information
NOFORN or NF	not releasable to foreign nationals
OCA	original classification authority
OIG DoD	Office of the Inspector General of the Department of Defense
PFPA	Pentagon Force Protection Agency

ACRONYM	MEANING
REL TO	releasable to
SCG	security classification guide
SNM	special nuclear material
U	Unclassified information
UCNI	unclassified controlled nuclear information
UD	unauthorized disclosure
U.S.C.	United States Code
USD(A&S)	Under Secretary of Defense for Acquisition and Sustainment
USD(I&S)	Under Secretary of Defense for Intelligence and Security
USD(R&E)	Under Secretary of Defense for Research and Engineering

G.2. DEFINITIONS.

Unless otherwise noted, these terms and their definitions are for the purpose of this issuance. Referenced definitions related to CUI in Section 2002.4 of Title 32, CFR can be found at https://intelshare.intelink.gov/sites/ousdi/hcis/sec/icdirect/information/CUI/Forms/AllItems.aspx.

TERM	DEFINITION
access	The ability or opportunity to acquire, examine, or retrieve CUI.
agency	Defined in Section 2002.4 of 32 CFR
aggregation	The creation of classified information from the accumulation of unclassified data or information from several areas within a document.
agreements and arrangements	Defined in Section 2002.4 of Title 32 CFR
authorized CUI holder	Defined in Section 2002.4 of Title 32 CFR
classified information	Defined in Section 2002.4 of Title 32 CFR
compilation	The creation of classified information resulting from the accumulation of unclassified data or information from several documents.

TERM	DEFINITION
contract	Defined in Section 252.204- 2008 and 7012 of the FARS/DFARS.
controlled environment	Defined in Section 2002.4 of Title 32 CFR
controls	Defined in Section 2002.4 of Title 32 CFR
CNSI	Defined in E.O. 13526.
CPM	Defined in Section 2002.4 of Title 32 CFR
CSAO	An official designated, in writing, by a DoD Component head who is responsible to the agency head for implementing the CUI Program. Also known as CUI SAO as defined in Section 2002.4 of Title 32 CFR
CTI	Defined in the DFARS 204.7301.
CUI	Defined in Section 2002.4 of Title 32 CFR
CUI Basic	Defined in Section 2002.4 of Title 32 CFR (DoD is not using this structure in its initial implementation phase.)
CUI category	Defined in Section 2002.4 of Title 32 CFR
CUI EA	Defined in Section 2002.4 of Title 32 CFR
CUI Indexes	An organizational grouping of CUI categories as defined by the CUI EA. The term was created by the CUI EA to replace the notion of a sub-category which implies a hierarchy structure or importance.
CUI misuse	Use of CUI in a manner not in accordance with the policy contained in E.O. 13556; Part 2002 of Title 32, CFR; the CUI Registry; agency CUI policy; or the applicable LRGWP governing the information.
CUI Program	Defined in Section 2002.4 of Title 32 CFR
CUI Registry	Defined in Section 2002.4 of Title 32 CFR
CUI Specified	Defined in Section 2002.4 of Title 32 CFR (DoD is not using this structure in its initial implementation phase.)
decontrol	Defined in Section 2002.18 of Title 32, CFR.

TERM	DEFINITION
Defense Industrial Base	Defined in the DoD Dictionary of Military and Associated Terms.
disseminating	Defined in Section 2002.4 of Title 32 CFR
document	Defined in Section 2002.4 of Title 32 CFR
DoD personnel	Defined in DoDI 5230.09.
foreign entity	Defined in Section 2002.4 of Title 32 CFR
formerly restricted data	Defined in Section 1045 of Title 10, CFR.
handling	Defined in Section 2002.4 of Title 32 CFR
lawful government purpose	Defined in Section 2002.4 of Title 32 CFR
LDC	Defined in Section 2002.4 of Title 32 CFR
legacy material	Defined in Section 2002.4 of Title 32 CFR
Limited Distribution	A legacy CUI category used by the National Geospatial-Intelligence Agency to identify a select group of sensitive, unclassified imagery or geospatial information and data created or distributed by National Geospatial Intelligence Agency or information, data, and products derived from such information (marked as LIMDIS and now referred to a GPI by CUI EA).
logical access	Electronic access controls authenticated through outside certificates accepted by the DoD to limit access to data files and systems only by vetted individuals.
misuse	Defined in Section 2002.4 of Title 32 CFR
NNPI	Information concerning the design, arrangement, development, testing, operation, administration, training, maintenance, and repair of the propulsion plants of naval nuclear powered ships and prototypes, including the associated nuclear support facilities.
non-Executive Branch entity	Defined in Section 2002.4 of Title 32 CFR

TERM	DEFINITION
personally identifiable information	Defined in Office of Management and Budget Circular No. A-130.
physical access	All DoD and non-DoD personnel entering or exiting DoD facilities or installations that authenticated a physical access control system (PACS).
portion	Defined in Section 2002.4 of Title 32 CFR
protection	Defined in Section 2002.4 of Title 32 CFR
public release	Defined in Section 2002.4 of Title 32 CFR
records	Defined in Section 2002.4 of Title 32 CFR
restricted data	Defined in Part 1045 of Title 10, CFR.
re-use	Defined in Section 2002.4 of Title 32 CFR
safeguarding	Prescribed measures and controls that protect classified information and CUI.
Senior Agency Official	An official appointed by the Secretary of Defense to be responsible for direction, administration, and oversight of the DoD's Information Security Program, including classification, declassification, CUI, safeguarding, and security education and training programs, and for the efficient and effective implementation of the guidance in this issuance.
SCG	Security classification guidance issued by an OCA identifying the elements of information regarding a specific subject requiring classification, and establishes the level and duration of classification for each element.
self-inspection	Defined in Section 2002.4 of Title 32 CFR
UD	Defined in Section 2002.4 of Title 32 CFR
unclassified	Information not requiring control, but requiring review before public release.

REFERENCES

Code of Federal Regulations, Title 10, Part 1045

Code of Federal Regulations, Title 32

Code of Federal Regulations, Title 36

Defense Federal Acquisition Regulation Supplement, Subparts 252.204-2008 and 7012, current edition

Deputy Secretary of Defense Memorandum, "Designation of Senior Agency Official for Controlled Unclassified Information," December 22, 2010

Deputy Secretary of Defense Memorandum, "Unauthorized Disclosures of Classified Information or Controlled Unclassified Information on DoD Information Systems," August 14, 2014

DoD Directive 5143.01, "Under Secretary of Defense for Intelligence (USD(I))," October 24, 2014, as amended

DoD Directive 5200.43, "Management of the Defense Security Enterprise," October 01, 2012, as amended

DoD Directive 5230.11, "Disclosure of Classified Military Information to Foreign Governments and International Organizations (NDP-1)," June 16, 1992

DoD Directive 5230.20, "Visits and Assignments of Foreign Nationals," June 22, 2005

DoD Directive 5400.07, "DoD Freedom of Information Act (FOIA) Program," April 5, 2019

DoD Instruction 2040.02, "International Transfers of Technology, Articles, and Services," March 27, 2014, as amended

DoD Instruction 3200.12, "DoD Scientific and Technical Information Program (STIP)," August 22, 2013, as amended

DoD Instruction 5015.02, "DoD Records Management Program," February 24, 2015, as amended

DoD Instruction 5200.02, "DoD Personnel Security Program (PSP), Change 2," March 21, 2014, as amended

DoD Instruction 5210.83, "DoD Unclassified Controlled Nuclear Information (UCNI)," July 12, 2012, as amended

DoD Instruction 5230.09, "Clearance of DoD Information for Public Release," January 25, 2019

DoD Instruction 5230.24, "Distribution Statements on Technical Documents," August 23, 2012, as amended

DoD Instruction 5230.29, "Security and Policy Review of DoD Information for Public Release," August 13, 2014, as amended

DoD Instruction 5400.04, "Provision of Information to Congress," March 17, 2009

DoD Instruction 5400.11, "DoD Privacy and Civil Liberties Programs," January 29, 2019

DoD Instruction 8320.07, "Implementing the Sharing of Data, Information, and Information Technology (IT) Services in the Department of Defense," August 03, 2015, as amended

DoD Instruction 8500.01, "Cybersecurity," March 14, 2014, as amended

DoD Instruction 8510.01, "Risk Management Framework (RMF) for DoD Information Technology (IT)," March 12, 2014, as amended

DoD Manual 5200.01, Volume 1, "DoD Information Security Program: Overview, Classification, And Declassification," February 24, 2012, as amended

DoD Manual 5200.01, Volume 2, "DoD Information Security Program: Marking of Information," February 24, 2012, as amended

DoD Manual 5200.45, "Instruction for Developing Security Classification Guides," April 02, 2013, as amended

DoD Manual 5400.07, "DoD Freedom of Information Act (FOIA) Program," January 25, 2017

Executive Order 13526, "Classified National Security Information," December 29, 2009

Executive Order 13556, "Controlled Unclassified Information," November 04, 2010

Federal Information Processing Standards Publication 199, "Standards for Security Categorization of Federal Information and Information Systems," February 2004

Federal Information Processing Standards Publication 200, "Minimum Security Requirements for Federal Information and Information Systems," March 2006

Information Security Oversight Office, "CUI Notice 2016-01: Implementation Guidance for the Controlled Unclassified Information Program," September 14, 2016

Information Security Oversight Office, "CUI Notice: Decontrolling Controlled Unclassified Information (CUI) in Response to a Freedom of Information Act (FOIA) Request," November 19, 2018

Information Security Oversight Office, "CUI Notice 2019-01: Controlled Unclassified Information (CUI) Coversheets and Labels," February 22, 2019

Information Security Oversight Office, "CUI Notice 2019-02: CUI Program Manage Position Description Template," May 13, 2019

Information Security Oversight Office, "CUI Notice 2019-03: Destroying Controlled Unclassified Information (CUI)," July 15, 2019

Information Security Oversight Office Response Letter to Under Secretary of Defense for Intelligence and Security, August 21, 2019

Information Security Oversight Office Response Letter to Under Secretary of Defense for Intelligence, Subject: "Unclassified versus Uncontrolled Unclassified Information", June 4, 2019

Intelligence Community Directive 710, "Classification Management and Control Markings System," June 21, 2013

Intelligence Community Policy Guidance 403.1, "Criteria for Foreign Disclosure and release of Classified National Intelligence," June 21, 2013

National Institute of Standards and Technology Special Publication 800-171, "Protecting Controlled Unclassified Information in Nonfederal Information Systems and Organizations," January 14, 2016, as amended

National Institute of Standards and Technology Special Publication 800-88, Revision 1, "Guidelines for Media Sanitization," February 5, 2015

National Strategy for Information Sharing and Safeguarding, December 19, 2012

Office of the Chairman of the Joint Chiefs of Staff, "DoD Dictionary of Military and Associated Terms," current edition

Office of the Chief of Naval Operations Instruction N9210.3, "Safeguarding of Naval Nuclear Propulsion Information (NNPI)," June 7, 2010

Office of Management and Budget Circular No. A-130, "Managing Information as a Strategic Resource," July 28, 2016

OPNAVINST N9210.3, "Safeguarding of Naval Nuclear Propulsion Information (NNPI)", June 07, 2010

Under Secretary of Defense for Intelligence Memorandum, "Controlled Unclassified Information Implementation and Oversight for the Defense Industrial Base," May 17, 2018

United States Code, Title 5

United States Code, Title 10

United States Code, Title 42, Chapter 14 (also known as the "Atomic Energy Act of 1954")

United States Code, Title 44

DoDI 5200.48

DoDI 5230.24 – Distribution Statements on DoD Technical Information

DoD INSTRUCTION 5230.24

DISTRIBUTION STATEMENTS ON DoD TECHNICAL INFORMATION

Originating Component:	Office of the Under Secretary of Defense for Research and Engineering
Effective:	January 10, 2023
Releasability:	Cleared for public release. Available on the Directives Division Website at https://www.esd.whs.mil/DD/.
Reissues and Cancels:	DoD Instruction 5230.24, "Distribution Statements on Technical Documents," August 23, 2012, as amended
Approved by:	Heidi Shyu, Under Secretary of Defense for Research and Engineering

Purpose: In accordance with the authority in DoD Directive (DoDD) 5137.02 and pursuant to Section 133a of Title 10, United States Code (U.S.C.), this issuance:

• Establishes policies, assigns responsibilities, and provides procedures for assigning distribution statements on technical information, including: research, development, test and evaluation (RDT&E); engineering; acquisition; and sustainment information, to denote the extent to which the technical information is available for secondary release and distribution without additional approvals or authorizations.

• Establishes a standard framework and markings for managing, sharing, safeguarding, and distributing technical information in accordance with national and operational security, privacy, records management, intellectual property, Federal procurement, and export-control policies, regulations, and laws.

• Aligns marking procedures for controlled technical information (CTI) in accordance with procedures described in DoD Instruction (DoDI) 5200.48 and Part 2002 of Title 32, Code of Federal Regulations (CFR).

• Helps originators of technical information determine to what extent it must be controlled in accordance with DoDD 5230.25.

TABLE OF CONTENTS

TABLES

FIGURES

SECTION 1: GENERAL ISSUANCE INFORMATION

1.1. APPLICABILITY.

This issuance:

a. Applies to:

(1) OSD, the Military Departments, the Office of the Chairman of the Joint Chiefs of Staff and the Joint Staff, the Combatant Commands, the Office of Inspector General of the Department of Defense, the Defense Agencies, the DoD Field Activities, and all other organizational entities within the DoD (referred to collectively in this issuance as the "DoD Components").

(2) Newly created, revised, or previously unmarked classified and unclassified technical information originated or managed by all DoD-funded RDT&E programs and DoD technical information originated or managed by DoD acquisition and sustainment activities, including system design, development, production, and procurement; sustainment, including logistics, maintenance, and materiel readiness; or collaboration activities.

(3) Newly created, revised, or previously unmarked information, whether in tangible (e.g., technical report, model, prototype, blueprint, photograph, plan, instruction, operating manual) or intangible form (e.g., technical service or visual description), including but not limited to:

(a) Engineering drawings.

(b) Configuration-management documentation.

(c) Engineering data and associated lists.

(d) Standards.

(e) Specifications.

(f) Technical manuals, reports, and orders.

(g) Blueprints, plans, and instructions.

(h) Computer software and computer software documentation.

(i) Catalog-item identifications.

(j) Data sets, studies and analyses, and other technical information that can be used or be adapted for use to design, engineer, produce, manufacture, operate, repair, overhaul, or reproduce any military or space equipment or technology concerning such equipment.

(k) Other types of technical data.

b. Does **not** apply to technical information categorized as cryptographic and communications security, communications, and electronic intelligence and such other categories that may be designated by the; Director, National Security Agency; Chief, Central Security Service; or the Under Secretary of Defense for Intelligence and Security.

c. May not be used by the DoD Components as authority to deny information to Congress or any Federal, State, or local government agency that requires such information for regulatory or other official government purposes. The DoD Component will notify the recipient when information is subject to DoD distribution controls.

d. Does not provide authority to withhold from public release unclassified information regarding DoD operations, policies, activities, or programs, including the costs and evaluations of performance and reliability of military and space equipment or any other information that is not exempt from release in accordance with DoDD 5400.07; DoDIs 5200.01, 5230.09, and 5230.29; DoD Manual (DoDM) 5200.01; or DoDM 5230.30.

1.2. POLICY.

The DoD will pursue a coordinated and comprehensive program to promote sharing technical information to the maximum extent possible to facilitate the efficient use of resources in accordance with safeguarding requirements as specified in national and DoD information and operations security policies, procurement regulations, policies, and procedures, including those related to competitive procurement, regulations, and laws specified in this issuance.

SECTION 2: RESPONSIBILITIES

2.1. DEPUTY CHIEF TECHNOLOGY OFFICER FOR SCIENCE AND TECHNOLOGY (DCTO(S&T)).

Under the authority, direction, and control of the Under Secretary of Defense for Research and Engineering, the DCTO(S&T) takes such actions that may be required to ensure consistent and appropriate implementation and control of technical information within this issuance's scope.

2.2. ADMINISTRATOR, DEFENSE TECHNICAL INFORMATION CENTER (DTIC).

Under the authority, direction, and control of the Under Secretary of Defense for Research and Engineering and in addition to the responsibilities in Paragraph 2.8., the Administrator, DTIC:

a. Acts as the DoD scientific and technical information program manager.

b. Maintains permanent documentation of controlling DoD office decisions for classifying and distributing technical information.

2.3. UNDER SECRETARY OF DEFENSE FOR ACQUISITION AND SUSTAINMENT.

The Under Secretary of Defense for Acquisition and Sustainment directs implementation of this issuance in accordance with DoDI 5000.90 to protect technical information developed or used within the Defense Acquisition System. Such implementation includes technology security and foreign disclosure reviews by appropriate authorities of technical information proposed for release to international partners or other external organizations.

2.4. UNDER SECRETARY OF DEFENSE FOR POLICY.

The Under Secretary of Defense for Policy:

a. Establishes DoD policy for international technology transfers, including, but not limited to, defense-related goods, services, and technologies.

b. Provides policy oversight of DoD activities relating to export controls and technology transfers.

c. Establishes and oversees the implementation of national and DoD policy for the disclosure of classified military information and foreign-engagement policy.

2.5. UNDER SECRETARY OF DEFENSE FOR INTELLIGENCE AND SECURITY.

The Under Secretary of Defense for Intelligence and Security:

a. Integrates the guidance in this issuance into the DoD information security and DoD operations security policies and programs, as applicable.

b. Exercises acquisition authority, as delegated by the Under Secretary of Defense for Acquisition and Sustainment, the Director of National Intelligence, or other appropriate official, for Intelligence, Counterintelligence, and Security technologies, systems, and equipment.

c. Ensures the exercise of acquisition authority by the heads of the Defense Intelligence, CI, and Defense Security Components is in coordination with the Under Secretary of Defense for Acquisition and Sustainment.

2.6. GENERAL COUNSEL OF THE DEPARTMENT OF DEFENSE.

The General Counsel of the Department of Defense advises the DoD Components regarding the statutory and regulatory requirements governing the export or other distribution of technical information.

2.7. DIRECTOR OF ADMINISTRATION AND MANAGEMENT.

The Director of Administration and Management:

a. Issues policy directing that the Washington Headquarters Services Defense Office of Prepublication and Security Review (DOPSR), or DoD Component public affairs personnel, properly review technical information submitted for public release clearance in accordance with DoDI 5230.09 to determine whether Distribution Statement A, as described in Paragraph 4.2.a., is appropriate for the technical information.

b. Processes appeals when public release is denied based upon this issuance, in accordance with DoDI 5230.29.

2.8. DOD COMPONENT HEADS.

The DoD Component heads:

a. Ensure that this issuance is implemented across their respective DoD Components in a uniform, consistent manner.

b. Ensure the Component's designation, handling, and decontrolling—including identification, sharing, marking, safeguarding, storage, distribution, and destruction—of controlled unclassified information (CUI) is in accordance with DoDI 5200.48.

c. Ensure that the controlling DoD office:

(1) Exercises its inherent U.S. Governmental responsibility to determine the appropriate marking of controlled technical information in accordance with this issuance, DoDI 5200.48, DoDI 5230.09, and DoDM 5200.01.

(2) Correctly marks and applies the appropriate distribution statement for all technical information regardless of media or form, including, but not limited to, RDT&E, sustainment, and logistics information.

d. Establish and maintain active education and training programs to provide a basic understanding of distribution statements and export-control markings and to inform personnel of their responsibilities for the proper handling and protection of marked technical information.

e. Ensure that managers of DoD technical programs assign distribution statements to all technical information originating in their programs.

f. Ensure that contractors and award recipients generating or holding CTI marked with Distribution Statements B through F comply with the cybersecurity requirements and export-control requirements directed by Clauses 252.204-7012 and 252.225-7048 of the Defense Federal Acquisition Regulation Supplement (DFARS), respectively.

g. Pursuant to Chapters 29, 31, and 33 of Title 44, U.S.C., and Subchapter B of Chapter XII of Title 36, CFR, ensure that all records created or received in accordance with this issuance, regardless of format or medium, are maintained and managed in accordance with DoD Component records management issuances and National Archives and Records Administration–approved dispositions to ensure proper maintenance, use, accessibility, and preservation.

h. Integrate operations security into DoD technical information distribution considerations to protect critical information and indicators associated with DoD technical information, in accordance with DoDD 5205.02E.

SECTION 3: PROCEDURES

3.1. GENERAL.

a. All DoD Components generating or responsible for technical information will determine who is authorized to access the information and apply the appropriate markings before primary distribution. Distribution statements will be used in addition to applicable classification markings pursuant to Volume 2 of DoDM 5200.01 and CUI markings pursuant to DoDI 5200.48.

b. DoD distribution statements are not required on technical proposals or similar documents submitted by contractors seeking DoD funds or contracts; however, markings specified by applicable acquisition regulations apply.

c. Distribution statements assigned to technical information by the controlling DoD office control secondary distribution in accordance with Volume 1 of DoDM 3200.14.

d. Technical information supporting acquisition, sustainment, logistics, maintenance, repair, supply, and RDT&E that is subject to the restrictions of this issuance will be marked, maintained, distributed, and controlled.

e. Unless otherwise authorized by the controlling DoD office, non-U.S. Government entities or individuals are strictly prohibited from further distributing technical information subject to the restrictions in this issuance.

f. All newly created, revised, or previously unmarked classified and unclassified DoD technical information will be assigned a distribution statement as described in Paragraph 4.2.

g. Distribution Statement X has been cancelled. Instead, use the export-control category described in Paragraph 4.3.e. Subsequent distribution of formerly Distribution Statement X information will display Distribution Statement C with export control as the stated reason for the marking.

h. Selection of the appropriate distribution statement is based on a number of considerations, including, but not limited to:

(1) Public release procedures specified in Enclosure 3 of DoDI 5230.29.

(2) Export controls in accordance with DoDD 5230.25; Parts 120–130 of Title 22, CFR (also known and referred to in this issuance as the International Traffic in Arms Regulations (ITAR)); and Parts 730–774 of Title 15, CFR (also known and referred to in this issuance as the Export Administration Regulations (EAR)).

(3) Export controls in accordance with Parts 110 and 810 of Title 10, CFR.

(4) Intellectual property and data-rights licenses for contract deliverables as described in Part 227 of the DFARS and the terms of the applicable transactional instrument.

(5) Relevant security classification guides, science and technology protection plans, program protection plans, and technology area protection plans as described in DoDI 5000.83.

i. Technical information in preliminary or working-draft form will be marked with a temporary notice or distribution statement pending proper security classification and distribution statement review as required by this issuance.

j. The first page or cover of any technical document will clearly display the distribution statement including the letter code and full statement described in Section 4, regardless of media or format.

(1) The distribution statement will appear in Block 12 of the Standard Form (SF) 298, "Report Documentation Page," available on the U.S. General Services Administration Website at https://www.gsa.gov/forms-library/report-documentation-page, in accordance with Volume 1 of DoDM 3200.14 and DFARS Clause 252.235-7011.

(2) If the technical information is not prepared in hard copy or paper form and is prepared digitally or in any medium that cannot practicably have a cover or title page, the appropriate distribution statement will be affixed to all physical and digital items by other means in as obvious a position as possible. Additionally, an oral presentation of the information, including voice recordings, will note the distribution statement.

k. Distribution statements will remain in effect until changed or removed by the controlling DoD office. Removal of or tampering with control markings by unauthorized personnel is strictly prohibited.

(1) If technical information has been declassified pursuant to Executive Order 13526 and the DoD Mandatory Declassification Review Program described in DoDM 5230.30, the distribution statement will be changed to reflect the final release determination.

(2) Technical information that has been reviewed pursuant to the Section 552 of Title 5, U.S.C. (also known as the Freedom of Information Act), and processed in accordance with DoDM 5400.07, and Section 2002.44(b) of Title 32, CFR, will be marked with a distribution statement to reflect the final release determination.

l. Each controlling DoD office will establish and maintain a procedure to review active and non-archived technical information for which it is responsible in order to increase availability when conditions permit. When release restrictions no longer apply, the controlling DoD office will obtain public-release determinations in accordance with DoDI 5230.09 and assign Distribution Statement A, cancel any other distribution statement, and notify DTIC and all known holders of the technical information of the change.

m. The controlling DoD office will notify DTIC, other known repositories and authorized holders promptly so that they can have an authoritative record of controlling DoD office decisions regarding classification and distribution when:

(1) The controlling DoD office's address changes.

(2) The controlling DoD office is redesignated.

(3) Classification markings, U.S. Government data-rights, distribution statements, or export-control warnings are changed or removed.

n. When possible or appropriate, those parts of a document that contain classified information or CTI will be prepared as an attachment, addendum, annex, enclosure, or similar removable section to allow separate distribution of the basic document at the lowest level of classification and to the widest possible audience.

o. Metadata describing technical information (e.g., title, abstract, keywords) will be written for the widest possible distribution in accordance with law, regulation, DoD policy, relevant security classification guides, science and technology protection plans, program protection plans, technology-area protection plans, or any other guidance pertaining to the withholding or release of technical information contained therein. When practical, metadata will be written in such a way that its content is unclassified and can be reviewed and determined by the DOPSR or the DoD Component public affairs personnel to be appropriate for Distribution Statement A.

p. Unclassified materials in any medium marked with Distribution Statement B, C, D, E, or F will be handled in accordance with procedures for banner marking, handling, storage, transmission, decontrol, and destruction described in DoDI 5200.48.

q. When no longer needed, CUI will be destroyed in accordance with DoDI 5200.48.

r. All records, regardless of format or medium, will be maintained and managed pursuant to National Archives and Records Administration–approved dispositions to ensure the proper maintenance, use, accessibility, and preservation.

3.2. PUBLIC RELEASE OF TECHNICAL INFORMATION.

a. DoDI 5230.09 requires a review of all DoD information before public release. Except as required by applicable Federal statutes or regulations or Executive orders, scientific and technical information resulting from unclassified fundamental research is exempt from prepublication controls and the review required by DoDI 5230.29.

b. Before submission to the DOPSR, DoD Components will ensure that all required preliminary reviews are conducted in accordance with DoDI 5230.29.

c. The DOPSR will approve for public release any official DoD information meeting the publication conditions of DoDI 5230.29. In accordance with DoDI 5230.29, DoD Component clearance authority may be delegated to the lowest level competent to evaluate the content and implications of public release of the information.

d. DoD technical information approved for public release will be marked "Distribution Statement A. Approved for public release: distribution unlimited."

e. Official DoD information, including, but not limited to, audio-visual materials or press releases that meet the criteria in DoDD 5122.05, will be coordinated through the Office of the Assistant to the Secretary of Defense for Public Affairs prior to public release.

3.3. CLASSIFIED TECHNICAL INFORMATION.

a. Classified technical information will be marked in accordance with Volume 2 of DoDM 5200.01 and assigned Distribution Statements B, C, D, E, or F. The distribution statement assigned to classified information will remain after declassification until the controlling DoD office changes or removes it.

b. If a classified document contains CTI, "CUI Warning Box for Classified Material" will appear on the first page of the document to alert readers to the presence of CUI. DoD Components will follow the format as described in DoDI 5200.48.

c. Declassified technical information that has no assigned distribution statement will be reviewed for possible CTI content and be handled as Distribution Statement E ("Distribution authorized to DoD Components only") until the controlling DoD office changes it.

d. Declassified technical information containing CTI will be marked with a "CUI Designation Indicator" on the first page of the document using the marking and format described in DoDI 5200.48.

e. Security classification guides will be marked in accordance with DoDM 5200.45.

3.4. UNCLASSIFIED CTI.

a. All unclassified CTI must be marked as CUI in accordance with DoDI 5200.48. DoD legacy material, including CTI, will not be required to be remarked or redacted while it remains under DoD control or is accessed online and downloaded for use within the DoD. However, any such information or new derivative information must be marked as CUI if a careful analysis determines that it qualifies as CUI.

b. Unclassified CTI originated by or under the control of the DoD will be marked with a distribution statement.

c. CUI that is not technical information as defined in the Glossary will be marked in accordance with DoDI 5200.48.

d. Procedures for marking DoD unclassified CTI align with the requirements of DoDI 5200.48. DoD-controlled unclassified technical information will include "CUI" in the banner and footer of each page and must include a distribution statement. The controlling DoD office will determine distribution availability in accordance with Paragraph 3.1.h. and select the appropriate reason and audience for the content.

e. The first page or cover of any document or material containing CTI will include a CUI designation indicator as described in DoDI 5200.48. The indicator will include:

(1) Controlled By.

Insert the name of the DoD Component unless the first page or cover is on letterhead stationery.

(2) Controlled By.

Insert the name of the DoD office.

(3) CUI Category.

For DoD unclassified CTI, the overarching CUI category authorizing the use of distribution statements is "CTI."

(4) Distribution Statement.

Insert the letter (B, C, D, E, or F) designating the appropriate distribution statement, described in Paragraph 4.2.

(5) Point of Contact.

Include the controlling DoD office's telephone number and/or office mailbox address. It is good practice to ensure that the telephone number and mailbox address are valid in case of personnel turnover.

f. Place the indicator at the bottom-right side of the first page or cover page, if applicable, of all technical information containing CUI, including classified material.

g. Directly beneath and separate from the CUI designation indicator box, affix the distribution statement in its entirety, including authorized audience, category, date of determination, and controlling DoD office. See Figures 1 and 2 for examples.

Figure 1. Example CUI Designation Indicator and Distribution Statement for CTI

Controlled By: OUSD(R&E) **Controlled By**: Defense Advanced Research Projects Agency **CUI Category**: CTI, Proprietary Business Information **Distribution Statement**: E **POC**: dod.component.mailbox@mail.mil

Figure 2. Example Distribution Statement for CTI

Distribution Statement E. Distribution authorized to DoD only; Proprietary Business Information; 18 OCT 2008. Other requests for this document must be referred to Defense Advanced Research Projects Agency, ATTN: TIO, 675 North Randolph Street Arlington, VA 22203-2114.

h. For newly originated, revised, or previously unmarked technical information, the controlling DoD office will determine whether the information contains export-controlled technical information. DoDD 5230.25, the ITAR, and the EAR provide guidance for making this determination. Personnel responsible for technology security, foreign disclosure, release reviews, or export-control analysis may provide additional guidance.

i. All information found to contain export-controlled technical information will be marked with the export-control warning in Paragraph 4.3.e.(2). Any information so marked must also be assigned Distribution Statement B, C, D, or E and specify "Export Controlled" as a reason for the assignment. This information must also include the notice to accompany the release of export-controlled data specified in DoDD 5230.25. Such information will be released only to entities qualified to receive export-controlled technical information.

j. All technical information delivered to the U.S. Government that includes contractor-owned proprietary data or other third-party intellectual property described in Section 5 will be clearly and legibly marked with the applicable data-rights markings as specified in Clause 252.227-7013, 252.227.7015, or 252.227-7018 of the DFARS, as applicable. The type of data-rights licenses that the U.S. Government holds will be a consideration when assigning distribution statements.

SECTION 4: DISTRIBUTION STATEMENTS FOR USE ON TECHNICAL INFORMATION

4.1. GENERAL.

a. Distribution statements will be shown on the title page or front cover of any technical document as described in Paragraph 3.1.j and on SF 298, where applicable. Compilations of documents may have different distribution statements governing their distribution if separated from the main document. The distribution statement applicable to the main document will be governed by the most restrictive distribution statement applicable to any part of the main document.

b. The wording of the distribution statements specified by this issuance may not be modified to accommodate additional distribution concerns such as distribution to foreign governments.

(1) Release or disclosure to foreign entities is outside the scope of secondary distribution as defined in the Glossary. Such release or disclosure must be in accordance with DoDD 5230.11 and DoDI 2040.02, as applicable.

(2) Where other markings are authorized and used in accordance with associated law, regulation, or U.S. Government–wide policy, those markings may be used to further inform distribution decisions in accordance with Paragraph 4.2. (e.g., releasable to ("REL TO")).

c. Distribution Statements B, C, D, and E are expressed in a standard format consisting of information in this order:

(1) Authorized audience.

(2) Defense category. This is the reason for the determination as to the extent to which the information is available for secondary release and distribution without additional approvals or authorizations. Categories are listed in Paragraph 4.3. Cite the category heading only, for example, "Controlled Technical Information."

(3) Date of determination.

(4) Controlling DoD office.

d. Up to three reasons or justifications for the non-release of technical information may apply. Therefore, more than one defense category may be cited in a distribution statement. In these instances, the most restrictive reason will govern the overall distribution determination.

e. At the discretion of the controlling DoD office, for purposes of clarification, Distribution Statements B, C, D, and E may begin with the word "Secondary," and the following text may precede the statement: "The [controlling DoD office] authorizes secondary distribution, release, and dissemination to the extent permitted by this distribution statement without additional approvals or authorizations."

4.2. DISTRIBUTION STATEMENTS AND NOTICES.

The distribution statements and notices described in this section are authorized for use on DoD technical information. A matrix of distribution statements and corresponding reasons appears in Table 1.

a. Distribution Statement A.

"Distribution Statement A. Approved for public release: distribution is unlimited."

(1) This statement may be used only on unclassified technical information that has been approved for public release by a competent authority in accordance with the procedures described in Paragraph 3.2.

(2) Scientific or technical information resulting from contracted fundamental research efforts will normally be assigned Distribution Statement A, except for those rare and exceptional circumstances where there is a likelihood of disclosing performance characteristics of military systems or of manufacturing technologies that are unique and critical to defense. Extramural research must be scoped and negotiated by the contracting/agreement activity with the contractor and research performer and determined in writing by the contracting/agreement officer to be fundamental research.

(3) This statement will not be used on classified technical information or information containing export-controlled technical information.

(4) This statement may not be used on technical information that was formerly classified or designated as CUI unless such information is approved for public release as described in Paragraph 3.2.

b. Distribution Statement B.

"Distribution Statement B. Distribution authorized to U.S. Government agencies [category] [date of determination]. Other requests for this document must be referred to [controlling DoD office]."

(1) This statement can apply to classified, CUI, and unclassified technical information.

(2) Distribution is authorized only to employees of U.S. Government Executive Branch departments and agencies and DoD Components.

c. Distribution Statement C.

"Distribution Statement C. Distribution authorized to U.S. Government agencies and their contractors [category] [date of determination]. Other requests for this document must be referred to [controlling DoD office]."

(1) This statement can apply to classified, CUI, and unclassified technical information.

(2) Distribution is authorized only to employees of U.S. Government Executive Branch departments and agencies and DoD Components, individuals, or employers who enter into a contract or award with the U.S. Government to perform a specific job, to supply labor and materials, or for the sale of products and services if such distribution is in furtherance of that contractual purpose.

d. Distribution Statement D.

"Distribution Statement D. Distribution authorized to the Department of Defense and U.S. DoD contractors only [category] [date of determination]. Other requests for this document must be referred to [controlling DoD office]."

(1) This statement can apply to classified, CUI, and unclassified technical information.

(2) Distribution is authorized only to military and civilian employees of the DoD or U.S. DoD contractors or grantees who enter into a contract or award with the DoD to perform a specific job, to supply labor and materials, or for the sale of products and services if such distribution is in furtherance of that contractual purpose.

e. Distribution Statement E.

"Distribution Statement E. Distribution authorized to DoD Components only [category] [date of determination]. Other requests for this document must be referred to [controlling DoD office]."

(1) This statement can apply to classified, CUI, and unclassified technical information.

(2) Distribution is authorized only to military personnel and civilian employees of the DoD.

(3) This statement will not be modified to further restrict access to specific branches or agencies within the DoD.

(4) Any technical information delivered to DTIC or any other DoD Component information center without a distribution statement will automatically be assigned Distribution Statement E.

f. Distribution Statement F.

"Distribution Statement F. Further distribution only as directed by [controlling DoD office] [date of determination] or higher DoD authority."

(1) This statement can apply to classified, CUI, and unclassified technical information.

(2) The controlling DoD office or a higher authority must be consulted before the material can be distributed. Use of this distribution statement cannot override distribution designated in Federal law, regulation, or U.S. Government–wide policy.

(3) To promote the free flow of information within the DoD, Distribution Statement F will not be used on classified, CUI, or unclassified scientific or technical information governed by the DoD scientific and technical information program described in DoDI 3200.12.

(4) Other technical information (e.g., technical manuals and orders, weapons, munitions documents) may be assigned Distribution Statement F, provided it will be reviewed on a 5-year cycle to consider a wider secondary distribution audience.

(5) The controlling DoD office must respond within 30 days to a request for release of technical information marked with Distribution Statement F. If the controlling DoD office agrees or there is no response within 30 days of receipt of a request to release the information, the information may be released to any DoD Component with Distribution Statement E and release must be documented.

g. REL TO Notice.

Information has been predetermined by the DoD controlling agency, in accordance with established foreign disclosure policies, to be releasable through established foreign disclosure procedures and channels to the foreign country or international organization indicated. The REL TO notice may be used to further inform distribution decisions. Follow the format described in Volume 2 of DoDM 5200.01.

4.3. DEFENSE CATEGORIES.

Defense categories describe the reasons for safeguarding or applying distribution controls to technical information. The listed defense categories override authorized reasons enacted in previous issuances but do not affect distribution statements assigned to legacy information in accordance with directives or instructions issued before the effective date of this issuance.

a. CTI.

CTI is a category of CUI. This is technical information with military or space application that is subject to controls on access, use, reproduction, modification, performance, display, release, disclosure, or distribution. It does not include information concerning general scientific, mathematics, or engineering principles commonly taught in schools, colleges, and universities or information in the public domain. Authorized distribution statements for CTI are Distribution Statements B, C, D, E, or F or REL TO.

b. Contractor Performance Evaluation.

This category protects information in management reviews, records of contract performance evaluation, or other advisory documents evaluating contractor programs, including supplier and product performance information in accordance with DoDI 5000.79. Authorized distribution statements for contractor performance evaluation are Distribution Statements B, E, or F.

c. Critical Technology.

This category protects information on technologies essential to the design, development, production, operation, application, or maintenance of an article or service that makes or could make a significant contribution to the military potential of any country, including the United States. Such information may be classified or unclassified and is export controlled. Authorized distribution statements for critical technology are Distribution Statements B, C, D, E, or F or REL TO.

d. Direct Military Support.

This category protects export-controlled technical information of such military significance that release for purposes other than direct support of DoD-approved activities may jeopardize an important technological or operational military advantage of the United States, another country, or a joint U.S.–foreign program. A competent authority will designate such data in accordance with DoDD 5230.25. Cover pages will be marked with the export-control warning shown in Figure 3 in accordance with Part 250 of Title 32, CFR. Authorized distribution statements for direct military support are Distribution Statements E or F or REL TO.

e. Export Controlled.

This category protects technical information in accordance with DoDD 5230.25, DoDI 2040.02, the ITAR, and EAR.

(1) Export-Controlled Technical Information.

Export-controlled technical information marked with Distribution Statement C or D will not be distributed outside the U.S. Government or to U.S. Government contractors without first verifying the recipient's eligibility and authority to receive export-controlled technical information by verifying that they have a current, valid Department of Defense Form 2345, "Militarily Critical Technical Data Agreement," available on the DoD Forms Management Program Website at https://www.esd.whs.mil/Portals/54/Documents/DD/forms/dd/dd2345.pdf, in accordance with DoDD 5230.25.

(2) Export-Control Warning.

All printed and electronic technical information, including technical information in a digital form, that is determined to contain export-controlled technical information, will be marked as shown in Figure 3. When it is technically impractical to use the entire statement, an abbreviated marking may be used and a copy of the full statement added to the notice to accompany the release of export-controlled technical information required by Part 250 of Title 32, CFR.

Figure 3. Export-Control Warning

WARNING - This document contains technical data whose export is restricted by the Arms Export Control Act (Section 2751 of Title 22, United States Code) or the Export Control Reform Act of 2018 (Chapter 58 Sections 4801-4852 of Title 50, United States Code). Violations of these export laws are subject to severe criminal penalties. Disseminate in accordance with provisions of DoD Directive 5230.25 and DoD Instruction 2040.02.

(3) Export-Control Distribution Statements.

Authorized distribution statements for export control are Distribution Statements B, C, D, E, or F or REL TO.

f. Foreign Government Information.

This category protects information provided to the United States by a foreign government or governments, an international organization of governments, or any element thereof with the express written requirement from the foreign government that the information, the source of the information, or both are not to be further distributed without the permission of the foreign entity. It also protects information produced by the United States pursuant to, or as a result of, a joint arrangement with a foreign government or governments, an international organization of governments, or any element thereof, with the express written requirement from the U.S. Government that the information, the arrangement, or both are to not to be further distributed without the permission of the U.S. Government. Authorized distribution statements for foreign government information are Distribution Statements B, C, D, E, or F or REL TO.

g. International Agreements (IAs).

This category protects IAs and IA-related information that may contain sensitive information not authorized for public release.

(1) This includes internal staffing documents, including, but not limited to, summary statements of intent, related technology security and foreign disclosure guidance, and IAs under negotiation.

(2) Although IAs, once established, are normally publicly released on the Department of State treaty portal, an IA containing sensitive information of a foreign government or international organization may be exempt from public release, as annotated in Section 130c of Title 10, U.S.C. Authorized distribution statements for such technical information are Distribution Statements B, C, D, E, or F or REL TO.

h. Operations Security.

This category protects technical information that that may be observed by adversary intelligence systems and to determine what indicators hostile intelligence systems may obtain that could be interpreted or assembled to derive critical information in time to be useful to adversaries. Authorized distribution statements for operations security are Distribution Statements B, E, or F.

i. Patents and Inventions.

This category protects information on any art or process—the way of doing or making things—that is or may be patentable under U.S. patent laws in which the U.S. Government owns or may own a right, title, or interest, including patents and patent applications under secrecy orders in accordance with Chapter 17 of Title 35, U.S.C. It also protects patentable information on systems or processes in the development or concept stage from premature distribution. This category does not apply to scientific or technical information protected by copyright or to patents issued by the U.S. Patent and Trademark Office, which are in the public domain. Authorized distribution statements for patents and inventions are Distribution Statements B, E, or F.

j. Proprietary Business Information.

This category protects material and information relating to, or associated with, a company's products, business, or activities, including but not limited to financial information, data or statements, trade secrets, product research and development, existing and future product designs, and performance specifications. Authorized distribution statements for proprietary information are Distribution Statements B, E, or F.

k. Small Business Innovation Research (SBIR).

The U.S. Government's rights to use, modify, reproduce, release, perform, display, or disclose this technical data are restricted by the DFARS and the terms of the applicable instrument. The cover will be marked with the SBIR data-rights marking in accordance with the applicable DFARS clause. Authorized distribution statements for SBIR technical information are Distribution Statements B, E, or F.

l. Software Documentation.

This category protects technical information relating to computer software that is releasable only in accordance with the software license in a contract, negotiated in accordance with Subpart 227.72 of the DFARS. It includes documentation such as user or owner manuals, installation instructions, operating instructions, and other information that explains the capabilities of or provides instructions for using or maintaining computer software. The documentation is releasable only in accordance with terms of the licensing agreement. Authorized distribution statements for software documentation are Distribution Statements B, C, D, E, or F.

m. Test and Evaluation.

This category protects results of testing and evaluation of commercial products or military hardware when disclosure may cause an unfair advantage or disadvantage to the product manufacturer. Authorized distribution statements for test and evaluation are Distribution Statements B, E, or F or REL TO.

n. Vulnerability Information.

This category protects technical information that provides insight into vulnerabilities of U.S. critical infrastructure, including DoD warfighting capabilities vital to national security that are otherwise not publicly available. Authorized distribution statements for vulnerability information are Distribution Statements B, C, D, E, or F.

Table 1. Distribution Statements and Their Corresponding Categories for Use

DISTRIBUTION STATEMENT A. Approved for public release: distribution is unlimited.					
DISTRIBUTION STATEMENT B. Distribution authorized to U.S. Government agencies [category] [date of determination]. Other requests for this document must be referred to [controlling DoD office].					
DISTRIBUTION STATEMENT C. Distribution authorized to U.S. Government agencies and their contractors [category] [date of determination]. Other requests for this document must be referred to [controlling DoD office].					
DISTRIBUTION STATEMENT D. Distribution authorized to Department of Defense and U.S. DoD contractors only [category] [date of determination]. Other requests for this document must be referred to [controlling DoD office].					
DISTRIBUTION STATEMENT E. Distribution authorized to DoD Components only [category] [date of determination]. Other requests for this document must be referred to [controlling DoD office].					
DISTRIBUTION STATEMENT F. Further distribution only as directed by [controlling DoD office] [date of determination] or higher DoD authority.					
REL TO. Information has been predetermined by the DoD controlling agency, in accordance with established foreign disclosure policies, to be releasable through established foreign disclosure procedures and channels, to the foreign country and international organization indicated.					
CATEGORY	A	B	C	D	E
PUBLIC RELEASE	X				
CTI		X	X	X	X
CONTRACTOR PERFORMANCE EVALUATION		X			X
CRITICAL TECHNOLOGY		X	X	X	X
DIRECT MILITARY SUPPORT					X
EXPORT CONTROLLED		X	X	X	X
FOREIGN GOVERNMENT INFORMATION		X	X	X	X
IAs		X	X	X	X
OPERATIONS SECURITY		X			X
PATENTS AND INVENTIONS		X			X
PROPRIETARY BUSINESS INFORMATION		X			X
SBIR		X			X
SOFTWARE DOCUMENTATION		X	X	X	X
TEST AND EVALUATION		X			X
VULNERABILITY INFORMATION		X	X	X	X

SECTION 5: THIRD PARTY–IMPOSED MARKINGS

5.1. GENERAL.

Generally, contractors retain ownership of their intellectual property and the technical and other data they develop (that it is embodied in) that is delivered or otherwise provided to the U.S. Government.

a. The U.S. Government typically receives license rights to use, reproduce, modify, release, perform, display, and disclose the information. The scope of the U.S. Government's license rights depends on a variety of factors, including the funding source for developing the technology, whether the information relates to a commercial item, and the parties' negotiations for specialized license terms or restrictions.

b. When the U.S. Government has unlimited rights, it may use, modify, reproduce, perform, display, release, or disclose information, in whole or in part, in any manner and for any purpose whatsoever and request or authorize others to do so.

5.2. RESTRICTIVE MARKINGS.

a. General.

Data rights markings that restrict the Government's use and distribution of technical data and software are authorized on technical data and software developed exclusively or partially at private expense except for certain categories of data in which the U.S. Government always has unlimited rights and data developed exclusively at U.S. Government expense. When the U.S. Government receives less than unlimited license rights in technical data, documents, or information, the contractor must mark the information with appropriate restrictive markings. The specific format and content of these markings depends on whether the data or software are commercial or noncommercial.

(1) For noncommercial technical data and noncommercial computer software, the applicable regulations specify the exact wording of the authorized restrictive markings.

(2) Commercial technical data and commercial computer software (except any commercial data that is not developed exclusively at private expense and certain categories of data in which the U.S. Government always has unlimited rights) may be marked with any restrictive marking that the owner of the data customarily provides the general public, provided it:

(a) Appropriately provides notice of the data owner's proprietary interests.

(b) Clearly characterizes the U.S. Government's license rights.

(c) Does not contravene Federal procurement law.

b. Procurement Contracts.

The Federal Acquisition Regulation and the DFARS govern the restrictive markings that apply to technical data, documents, or information that is developed or delivered under a procurement contract. Subpart 227.71 of the DFARS governs the license rights and restrictive markings for technical data, and Subpart 227.72 of the DFARS governs computer software and its documentation.

(1) Noncommercial Technologies.

The DFARS governs the restrictive markings that apply to technical data, documents, or information that are developed or delivered under DoD procurement contracts. DFARS Subpart 227.71 addresses the license rights and restrictive markings for technical data, and Subpart 227.72 of the DFARS addresses license rights in computer software and computer software documentation, which is considered a category of technical data. Restrictive markings that restrict the Government's use and distribution of technical data and software are authorized for noncommercial technical data and noncommercial computer software developed and delivered under U.S. Government procurement contracts with less than unlimited rights.

The DFARS establishes specific procedures governing the placement and location of restrictive markings on deliverables, storage media, and transmittal documents and markings to be used. There are only seven types of markings related to restrictions on the Government's use and distribution of technical data and software that are authorized for use on noncommercial technical data and noncommercial computer software by the relevant clauses:

(a) The Government Purpose Rights marking authorized by Clause 252.227-7013 of the DFARS.

(b) The Limited Rights marking, for technical data only, authorized by Clause 252.227-7013 of the DFARS.

(c) The Restricted Rights marking, for computer software only, authorized by Clause 252.227-7014 of the DFARS.

(d) The Special License Rights marking authorized by Clause 252.227-7013 of the DFARS.

(e) The Special License Rights marking authorized by Clause 252.227-7014 of the DFARS.

(f) The SBIR marking authorized by Clause 252.227-7018 of the DFARS.

(g) Pre-existing markings authorized under a prior U.S. Government contract.

(2) Commercial Technologies.

The DFARS guidance concerning restrictive markings on commercial technologies is flexible to account for the variations in markings customarily used in the marketplace provided to the public.

(a) The U.S. Government's license rights will be the standard Limited Rights specified in Clause 252.227-7015 of the DFARS for commercial technical data (except any commercial data not developed exclusively at private expense and certain categories of data in which the U.S. Government always has unlimited rights).

(b) Similarly, the DFARS does not specify a restrictive marking for commercial computer software. Commercial computer software delivered to the Government will be marked consistent with the license customary provided by the owner to the public, provided it is clear and doesn't contravene U.S. Government law. The U.S. Government may negotiate specifically negotiated license rights, which will be documented in the contract, if the commercial rights do not suffice. Any commercial computer software developed exclusively or partially at U.S. Government expense will be marked with the appropriate marking in Clause 252.227-7014 of the DFARS.

c. Instruments Other Than Federal Acquisition Regulation-Based Contracts.

Technical data, documents, or information may be developed or delivered to the U.S. Government under various legally binding instruments other than Federal Acquisition Regulation-based contracts. Examples include grants, cooperative agreements, cooperative research and development agreements pursuant to Section 3710a of Title 15, U.S.C., or other transaction agreements pursuant to Section 4201 of Title 10, U.S.C. The legally binding agreement should establish the U.S. Government's license rights and any specified marking.

d. Other Forms of Proprietary Information.

The U.S. Government may receive a private entity's proprietary information in a variety of contexts in which there may not be a formal legal agreement to document the U.S. Government's license rights or any specific restrictive markings. For example, a private entity may provide the U.S. Government with certain technical information to supplement the U.S. Government's evaluation of a new technology for market research or similar activities. In these cases, the restrictive marking on the materials may be the key element in identifying the U.S. Government's license rights in those materials. Use caution when evaluating these materials for applying of the appropriate distribution statement to ensure that the private entities' proprietary interests are protected.

e. Copyright.

Although not necessarily used as a restrictive marking, a notice of copyright may be used in addition to the other authorized markings. Conforming notices are limited to including the owner's legal name, copyright year, and either the term "copyright," the abbreviation "CopyR," or the copyright symbol, "©."

(1) A conforming copyright notice alone does not qualify as a restrictive marking.

(2) The contracting officer cannot accept third-party copyrighted material (i.e., copyrights in an entity's name that is not the prime contractor) without ensuring that the prime contractor obtained a license in that third-party copyrighted material consistent with the U.S. Government's license rights in the data.

(3) Copyright protection is not available in the United States for works created by U.S. Government employees as part of their official duties except when a civilian member of the faculty of certain listed U.S. Government institutions owns the copyright to certain works in accordance with Section 105 of Title 17, U.S.C.

5.3. REVIEWING THE APPLIED MARKINGS.

Technical data, documents, or information marked with contractor-imposed restrictive markings may be released only in accordance with U.S. Government license rights in those materials.

a. Step 1.

Verify the U.S. Government's license rights or authorization to distribute. A third party–imposed restrictive marking provides general notice of restrictions on the use or disclosure of the information but may not completely or accurately specify the entire spectrum of license rights granted to the U.S. Government. In most cases, the DFARS clauses in the contract (or language in other types of agreements like grants, other transactions, etc.) dictate the exact language for license rights markings with the exception of markings for commercial computer software.

b. Step 2.

Apply the markings. The appropriate distribution statement is dependent in part on the scope of the U.S. Government's license rights in those materials.

(1) In most cases, the reason "Proprietary Business Information" will provide a basis for Distribution Statements B, E, or F. When used as the reason for a limitation, note the U.S. Government's license rights as described in Paragraph 5.2.a.(1) in parentheses (e.g., "Proprietary Information (DFARS Limited Rights)," "Proprietary Information (SBIR Rights)").

(2) If the U.S. Government has unlimited rights in the information, the materials may qualify for Distribution Statement A if no other reason exists for using a more restrictive distribution statement or other restrictive markings (e.g., classification, export control) prevent public dissemination and after appropriate clearance procedures are carried out in accordance with DoDI 5230.29. A copyright notice alone does not necessarily qualify as a restrictive marking.

c. Step 3.

Implement appropriate procedures and safeguards governing distribution. In some cases, the U.S. Government may be authorized to distribute proprietary information only when the release or disclosure accompanies certain procedural safeguards. For example, the U.S. Government may release or disclose technical data or computer software governed by a DFARS Government Purpose Rights license only when the recipient of the information has signed a nondisclosure agreement as specified in DFARS 227.7103-7 or receives the information under performance of a contract in accordance with DFARS Clause 252.227-7025. The U.S. Government must ensure that these requirements are satisfied before distribution.

GLOSSARY

G.1. ACRONYMS.

ACRONYM	MEANING
CFR	Code of Federal Regulations
CTI	controlled technical information
CUI	controlled unclassified information
DCTO(S&T)	Deputy Chief Technology Officer for Science and Technology
DFARS	Defense Federal Acquisition Regulation Supplement
DoDD	DoD directive
DoDI	DoD instruction
DoDM	DoD manual
DOPSR	Defense Office of Prepublication and Security Review
DTIC	Defense Technical Information Center
EAR	Export Administration Regulations
IA	international agreement
ITAR	International Traffic in Arms Regulations
RDT&E	research, development, test, and evaluation
SBIR	small business innovation research
SF	standard form
U.S.C.	United States Code

G.2. DEFINITIONS.

Unless otherwise noted, these terms and their definitions are for the purpose of this issuance.

TERM	DEFINITION
authorized holder	Individual, agency, organization, or group of users permitted to designate or handle classified information or CUI.
budget activity	Defined in Chapter 1 of Volume 2A of DoD 7000.14-R.
computer software	Computer programs, source codes, source code listings, object code listings, design details, algorithms, processes, flow charts, formulas, and related material that would enable the software to be reproduced,

recreated, or recompiled. Computer software does not include computer databases or computer software documentation.

configuration management documentation Documentation that is prepared by a design activity for the disclosure and description of configuration items, form, fit, function, interface, performance, operation, reliability, maintainability, quality control, or other configuration management or engineering documentation features of items, materials, methods, practices, processes, and services.

contracted fundamental research Research performed under grants and contracts that are funded by RDT&E Budget Activity 1 (Basic Research), whether performed by universities or industry, and Budget Activity 2 (Applied Research) performed on campus at a university. The research will not be considered fundamental in those rare and exceptional circumstances where the applied research–funded effort presents a likelihood of disclosing performance characteristics of military systems or manufacturing technologies that are unique and critical to defense and where the contract or grant records agreement on restrictions.

contractor An individual or organization outside the U.S. Government that enters into any type of contractual vehicle (e.g., a contract, agreement, order, other transaction) to provide any supplies or services, including, but not limited to, research and development, to a U.S. Government agency, including prime contractors and subcontractors.

controlling DoD office The DoD activity that sponsored the work that originated the technical information for the DoD and has the inherently governmental responsibility for determining the dissemination of such technical information. For joint sponsorship, the controlling DoD office is determined by agreement and may be a party, group, or committee representing the interested activities or DoD Components. The DoD activity that manages technical information not originated for the DoD but managed by that DoD activity has the inherently governmental responsibility for determining the dissemination of that technical information. Only the controlling DoD office or higher DoD authority may authorize dissemination beyond the dissemination statement.

critical technology Defense articles or defense services included in the ITAR.

Items included in Supplement No. 1 to Part 774 of EAR and controlled:

Pursuant to multilateral regimes, including for reasons relating to national security, chemical and biological weapons proliferation, nuclear nonproliferation, or missile technology; or
For reasons relating to regional stability or surreptitious listening.
Specially designed and prepared nuclear equipment, parts and components, materials, software, and technology covered by Part 810 of Title 10, CFR.

Nuclear facilities, equipment, and material covered by Part 110 of Title 10, CFR.

Select agents and toxins covered by Part 331 of Title 7, CFR; Part 121 of Title 9, CFR; or Part 73 of Title 42, CFR.

Emerging and foundational technologies controlled pursuant to Chapter 58 of Title 50, U.S.C.

Items listed on the DoD critical technologies list pursuant to Section 1049 of Public Law 115-232.

CTI Technical information with military or space applications that is subject to controls on access, use, reproduction, modification, performance, display, release, disclosure, or distribution. CTI does not include information concerning general scientific, mathematics, or engineering principles commonly taught in schools, colleges, and universities or information in the public domain.

CUI Defined in Section 2002.4 of Title 32, CFR.

CUI category Defined in Section 2002.4 of Title 32, CFR.

date of determination The date on which the reason for assigning a specific distribution statement was determined. It is usually the date of the report but may be earlier if a contract or other agreement specifies it. The date is important for document identification and for legal, contractual, and regulatory evidentiary purposes.

Defense Acquisition System Defined in DoDD 5135.02.

defense article Defined in Part 120.6 of the ITAR.

defense service Defined in Part 120.9 of the ITAR.

distribution statement A statement used to mark technical information to indicate the extent of its availability for secondary distribution, release, and disclosure

	without additional approvals or authorizations. A distribution statement marking is distinct from and in addition to a security classification marking assigned in accordance with Volume 2 of DoDM 5200.01.
document	Defined in Section 2002.4 of Title 32, CFR.
engineering information	Engineering data used for design, development, test, manufacture, acceptance, training, operation, maintenance, and overhaul. The principal types of engineering information are engineering drawings and associated lists (e.g., parts list, data list, index list), manufacturer specifications and standards, data sheets, test reports, bills of material, handbooks, technical orders or manuals, engineering changes, technical data packages, and other documents that provide data on reliability, maintainability, end-item application, and quality control.
export control	Defense articles, defense services, and related technical data subject to the ITAR or commodities, software, or technology subject to the EAR.
export-controlled technical information	Technical information concerning certain items, commodities, technology, software, or other information whose export could reasonably be expected to adversely affect U.S. national security and nonproliferation objectives, including technical data defined in Section 120.10 of Title 22, CFR, and technology defined in Part 772.1 of Title 15, CFR, and Section 4801(11) of Title 50, U.S.C.
extramural research	Research conducted by any research institution other than the Federal agency to which the funds supporting the research were appropriated.
foreign government information	Information provided to the U.S. Government by a foreign government or governments, an international organization of governments, or any element thereof with the expectation that the information, the source of the information, or both are to be held in confidence and afforded the same degree of protection afforded to U.S. Government information of an equivalent classification and distribution control as required by national security regulations; or Information produced by the U.S. Government pursuant to or as a result of a joint arrangement with a foreign government or governments, an international organization of governments, or any element thereof requiring that the information, the arrangement, or both are to be held in confidence and afforded the same degree of protection afforded to U.S. Government information of an equivalent

	classification and distribution control as required by national security regulations.
fundamental research	Defined in National Security Decision Directive-189.
legacy material	Defined in Section 2002.4 of Title 32, CFR.
primary distribution	The initial targeted distribution of or access to technical documents authorized by the controlling DoD office or any release by the controlling DoD office thereafter.
proprietary	Information relating to or associated with a company's products, business, or activities, including, but not limited to, financial information, data or statements, trade secrets, product research and development, existing and future product designs and performance specifications, marketing plans or techniques, schematics, client lists, computer programs, processes, and knowledge that have been clearly identified and properly marked by the company as proprietary information, trade secrets, or company confidential information.
RDT&E	Defined in Chapter 1 of Volume 2A of DoD 7000.14-R.
repository	Data centers, information analysis centers, technical libraries, and other information activities that collect, store, process, and provide document, data, or information services.
secondary distribution	Release of technical information by an entity other than the originator or controlling DoD office. This includes loaning, allowing the reading of, or releasing a document outright in whole or in part.
technical data	Defined in Clause 252.227-7013(a)(15) of the DFARS.
technical document	Any recorded information that conveys scientific and technical information or technical data. This includes informal documents like working papers, memorandums, and preliminary reports when such documents have use beyond the immediate mission requirement or will become part of the historical record of technical achievements.
technical information	Technical data or computer software of any kind that can be used or adapted for use in the design, production, manufacture, assembly, repair, overhaul processing, engineering, development, operation, maintenance, adapting, testing, or reconstruction of goods or materiel or any technology that advances the state of the art, or establishes a new art, in an area of significant military applicability in the United States. The data may be in tangible form, such as a blueprint,

photograph, plan, instruction, or an operating manual or may be intangible, such as a technical service or oral, auditory, or visual descriptions. Examples of technical data include research and engineering data, engineering drawings, and associated lists; specifications; standards; process sheets; manuals; technical reports; technical orders; catalog-item identifications; data sets; studies, analyses, and related information; and computer software.

unclassified Defined in DoDI 5200.48.

DoDI 5230.24

References

Code of Federal Regulations, Title 10

Code of Federal Regulations, Title 15

Code of Federal Regulations, Title 22

Code of Federal Regulations, Title 32

Code of Federal Regulations, Title 36, Chapter XII, Subchapter B

Code of Federal Regulations, Title 42, Part 73

Code of Federal Regulations, Title 7, Part 331

Code of Federal Regulations, Title 9, Part 121

Defense Federal Acquisition Regulation Supplement, current edition

DoD 7000.14-R, Volume 2A, Chapter 1, "Department of Defense Financial Management Regulations: Budget Formulation and Presentation," current edition

DoD Directive 5122.05, "Assistant to the Secretary of Defense for Public Affairs (ASD(PA))," August 7, 2017

DoD Directive 5135.02, "Under Secretary of Defense for Acquisition and Sustainment (USD(A&S))," July 15, 2020

DoD Directive 5137.02, "Under Secretary of Defense for Research and Engineering (USD(R&E))," July 15, 2020

DoD Directive 5205.02E, "DoD Operations Security (OPSEC) Program," June 20, 2012, as amended

DoD Directive 5230.11, "Disclosure of Classified Military Information to Foreign Governments and International Organizations," June 16, 1992

DoD Directive 5230.25, "Withholding of Unclassified Technical Data from Public Disclosure," November 6, 1984, as amended

DoD Directive 5400.07, "DoD Freedom of Information Act (FOIA) Program," April 5, 2019

DoD Instruction 2040.02, "International Transfers of Technology, Articles, and Services," March 27, 2014, as amended

DoD Instruction 3200.12, "DoD Scientific and Technical Information Program (STIP)," August 22, 2013, as amended

DoD Instruction 5000.79, "Defense-wide Sharing and Use of Supplier and Product Performance Information (PI)," October 15, 2019

DoD Instruction 5000.83, "Technology and Program Protection to Maintain Technological Advantage," July 20, 2020, as amended

DoD Instruction 5000.90, "Cybersecurity for Acquisition Decision Authorities and Program Managers," December 31, 2020

DoD Instruction 5200.01, "DoD Information Security Program and Protection of Sensitive Compartmented Information (SCI)," April 21, 2016, as amended

DoD Instruction 5200.48, "Controlled Unclassified Information (CUI)," March 6, 2020

DoD Instruction 5230.09, "Clearance of DoD Information for Public Release," January 25, 2019, as amended

DoDI 5230.24

DoD Instruction 5230.29, "Security and Policy Review of DoD Information for Public Release," August 13, 2014, as amended

DoD Manual 3200.14, Volume 1, "Principles and Operational Parameters of the DoD Scientific and Technical Information Program (STIP): General Processes," March 14, 2014, as amended

DoD Manual 5200.01, "DoD Information Security Program," February 24, 2012, as amended

DoD Manual 5200.45, "Instructions for Developing Security Classification Guides," April 2, 2013, as amended

DoD Manual 5230.30, "DoD Mandatory Declassification Review (MDR) Program," December 22, 2011, as amended

DoD Manual 5400.07, "DoD Freedom of Information Act (FOIA) Program," January 25, 2017

Executive Order 13526, "Classified National Security Information," December 29, 2009

National Security Decision Directive-189, "National Policy on the Transfer of Scientific, Technical, and Engineering Information," September 21, 1985

Public Law 115-232, Section 1049, "John S. McCain National Defense Authorization Act for Fiscal Year 2019," August 13, 2018

United States Code, Title 5, Section 552, (also known as the Freedom of Information Act)

United States Code, Title 10

United States Code, Title 15

United States Code, Title 17, Section 105

United States Code, Title 22

United States Code, Title 35, Chapter 17

United States Code, Title 44

United States Code, Title 50

www.ingramcontent.com/pod-product-compliance
Lightning Source LLC
Chambersburg PA
CBHW062133020426
42335CB00013B/1195

* 9 7 9 8 9 8 9 1 0 3 7 9 9 *